TREE ANATOMY

CONNECTIONS

SHIGO AND TREES, ASSOCIATES
P.O. BOX 769, DURHAM, NH 03824

TREE ANATOMY

BY

ALEX L. SHIGO

Former chief scientist and leader of a Pioneering Project on Discoloration and Decay in Forest Trees, U.S. Forest Service.

Dedication
To
Marilyn

The Author - Alex L. Shigo was born in Duquesne, Pennsylvania on May 8, 1930. He received his BS in Biology from Waynesburg College in 1956 and his MS and Ph.D. in Plant Pathology from West Virginia University in 1958 and 1960, respectively. From 1959 to 1985 he was employed by the U.S. Forest Service as chief scientist and Project Leader of a Pioneering Project on Discoloration and Decay in Forest Trees. He has dissected over 15,000 trees with a chainsaw. He has studied trees in many countries. His research yielded 270 publications and he has received many honors and awards. He believes that we must help trees by helping the people who work with trees by providing sound educational programs based on research.

ACKNOWLEDGMENTS

THANKS go to many people who helped make this book possible: Way Hoyt for samples and information on tropical trees, Steve Nimz for samples of trees from Hawaii, Sam Knapp, John Phillips, and Robert Phillips for samples of trees from California, John Martin for samples of trees from South Carolina and The Fairchild Tropical Gardens in Miami, Florida for samples of tropical trees. For review of the book, I thank Dr. Kevin T. Smith, Plant Physiologist, U.S. Forest Service, Dr. Linn Bogle, Plant Anatomist, University of New Hampshire, and Kenneth R. Dudzik, Forester, U.S. Forest Service. I thank my wife Marilyn for typing the manuscript and for many helpful comments for improvement of the manuscript. I thank Everett Rowley from Sherwin Dodge Printers of Littleton, NH for many helpful suggestions for improving the manuscript.

Front cover - Iodine staining shows starch behind buds of Colorado blue spruce dissected in the fall (Page 14).

Back cover - Woody root growing from a meristematic point in an American beech root (Page 67).

Printed in USA by Sherwin/Dodge, Littleton, NH

ISBN: 0-943563-14-3

FLOWERS AND FRUIT

Witch Hazel, *Hamamelis virginiana*
Perfect flowers with stamens (male) and carpels (female) parts.
The line at the lower right of each photograph is the width, in millimeters, of the field of view before photographic enlargement.

Trees. Majestic. Beautiful. Big. Tall. Long-Lived.

Thousands of books show and discuss the majesty and beauty of trees. From the outside, and usually from a distance. The purpose of this book is to show and discuss the majesty and beauty of trees also. But, from the inside, and from close-up views.

Trees are plants that are woody, perennial, shedding, and highly compartmented. Trees usually have a central stem over 3 meters tall, whereas woody shrubs usually have several stems less than 3 meters tall. Some woody shrubs are shown in this book. The information given here is also applicable to woody shrubs.

Trees are connected with many other communities of organisms. The connections benefit the long-term, high-quality survival of all members of the natural living system.

TREE ANATOMY IS THE SCIENCE OF THE PARTS AND STRUCTURES OF THE TREE SYSTEM. THIS BOOK GIVES A CLOSER LOOK AT THE PARTS AND STRUCTURES OF THE TREE SYSTEM.

TABLE OF CONTENTS

Hazelnut, *Corylus americana*
Male and female parts are in separate flowers on the same plant. The male flowers make up a catkin or ament (left). This species is a woody shrub. Other species are moderate-sized trees.

The photographs in this book were selected from over 3000 that were made over a 3-year period.

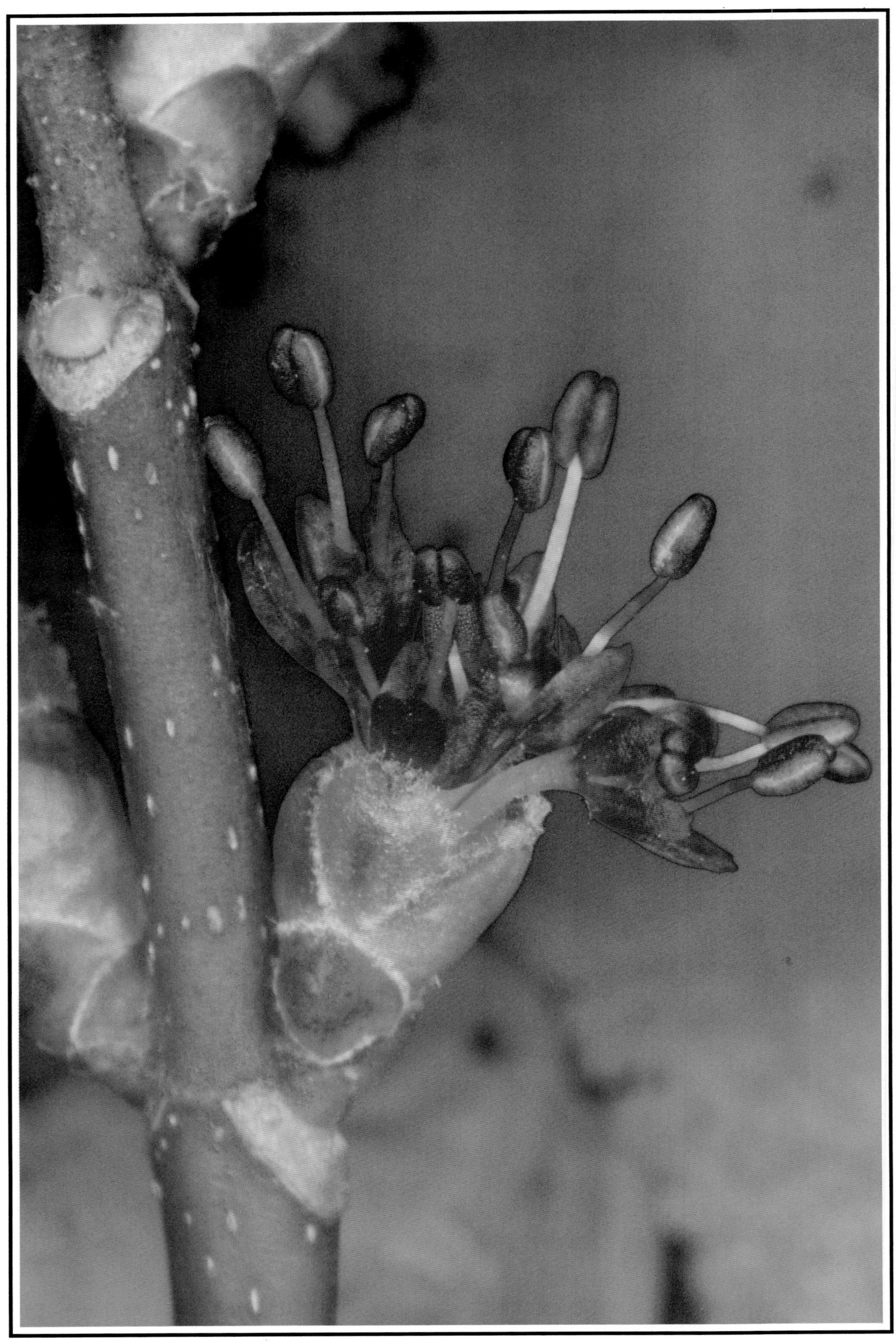

Red maple, *Acer rubrum*
Male flowers. The 4-lobed anthers have not yet released their pollen.

Red Maple, *Acer rubrum*
Female flowers with developing winged fruits containing seeds.

REPRODUCTION
The real beauty of flowers lies in their ability to repeat the species.

ENERGY
Energy stored the previous growth period is required for growth of early blossoming flowers.

Monoclinous - perfect flowers with functional stamens and ovaries.
Diclinous - imperfect flowers with functional stamens (male) only, or functional ovaries (female) only.
Monoecious - male and female flowers on the same tree.
Dioecious - male and female flowers on separate trees.
Polygamous -the tree has some combination of male, female, and perfect flowers. Some examples are *Acer* species, *Bursera simaruba* and *Myrsine floridana*.

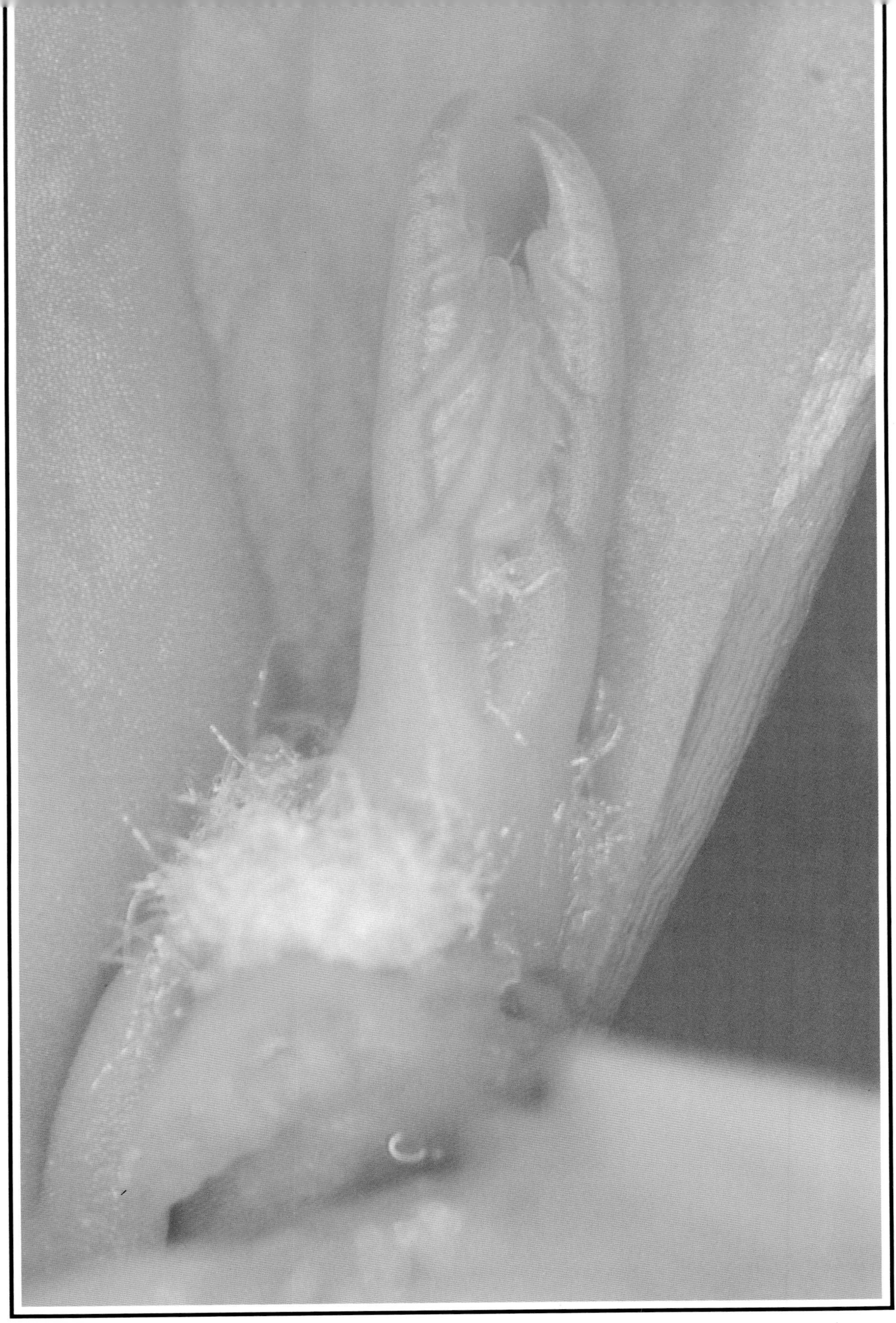

Norway maple, ***Acer platanoides***

New life starts with the embryo in the seed. Some seeds, such as those of the maples, may begin to grow soon after they fall from the tree onto a suitable site. Other seeds may not begin to grow until they pass through a period of cold, or after the heat of a fire opens a cone and releases the seeds. Mangrove seeds have a spear-like radicle that forms while the seed is still on the tree. When the seed drops, the radicle usually penetrates the mud, and the root takes hold.

Reproduction is a high energy-requiring process.

THE ANATOMY OF THE TREE SYSTEM

Tree systems are intelligent. Intelligent in the sense of having the ability to connect and use genetic information in ways that ensure continuous high-quality survival of all the connected members of the system. This book is a brief introduction to some of the parts and structures of the tree system.

I have tried to select subjects not usually discussed in other books and to present them in ways not usually seen in other books — large color photographs. I encourage readers to study other books on plant biology, botany, and wood anatomy for more details on the subjects.

Trees are receiving more and more attention worldwide. Concerns are for forests, urban trees, trees for medicinal purposes, and the list goes on and on. People are talking about trees, treating trees that have problems, and writing about processes in trees. My concern is that many of these activities are going on without a basic understanding of what trees really are and how trees function. A super-simplistic view of trees serves as the basis for much of the attention being given to trees. Myths, misconceptions, and half-truths about trees are more the rule than the exception. A major reason for so many myths, misconceptions, and half-truths is that trees are so tall and massive, that systematic dissections to understand tree anatomy are physically difficult. Chainsaws, axes, and other large tools are needed. These tools are not considered as research tools. And when tree sections are studied, cross sections are usually viewed. Yes, they are important, but not as important as longitudinal radial sections. Such longitudinal dissections are rarely done. I have shown and discussed large tree dissection in my book, **A New Tree Biology.**

TREE ANATOMY focuses on another problem area with tree anatomy. Wood sections prepared in various ways and cut on a microtome are extremely common and can be easily found in many books. Microtome sections may also show artifacts because they are cut so thin and because they are fixed in many materials. For example, tyloses are often absent from microtome sections of wood that contain tyloses. Yes, information from such sections is very valuable, especially to those who work with wood products. But, for living trees other methods must be used. Here I focus on low magnification of tree parts. To prepare the samples, large sharp knives and razor blades served as the main tools. And, again, these are not high on the list of research tools. Last, but not the least, are the pick and shovel for digging roots. And especially for digging roots in frozen soils. These were the tools and methods that were used to make this book.

HOW TO USE THIS BOOK

Start by slowly leafing through the book several times. Get a "feel" for the beauty and majesty of the tree system. Think of the book as a new piece of music. The more you hear the music and become a part of it, the more you *hear into* the music and it becomes a part of you. So it should be with this book.

Then begin to read only the major captions to learn the subjects. Again, go through the book several times this way until all the subjects connect in your mind. Next, read the text and connect it with each photo. Do only a few at a time. Finally, take time to study each photo to see how much you *can see* in each photo, especially the many details that are not mentioned in the text.

HOW TO BENEFIT FROM THIS BOOK

This book can help you to move your mind's eye to the top of tall trees to view tiny flowers and leaves, and into trunks to view living cells, and into the soil to see the fungi at work, even when the snow is deep and the wind is cold. Once this wonderful connection begins to happen you will speak differently about trees. You will begin to base treatments on understanding rather than on myths.

TREES ARE FORGIVING

Trees in forests, cities, parks, and orchards receive a great amount of abuse. Much of the abuse is not intentional. It is done usually because of ignorance. And, because the tree is so forgiving and does not die, the treatment or other abusive actions are thought to be good for the tree. However, as the abuses continue, the tree does reach a point, a threshold, where any additional abusive action leads to a noticeable decline or death of a part of the tree, or the entire tree may begin to decline. At this point, it is usually too late for any remedial action because a tree is a generating system. Being a generating system is the advantage a tree has when it is young and this is a major reason why the tree is so forgiving. To generate new parts requires energy, lots of energy. As the tree begins to lose its ability to trap the sun's energy and to absorb essential elements from the soil, noticeable problems start. I say "noticeable problems" because the problems are usually there long before most people do notice them. By the time they are noticed, it is usually too late to help the tree. Yet, over and over again this is the time people call for help.

How does all this fit into a book on tree anatomy? The answer is that if more people understand the parts and structures of the tree system better, and the ways they function, the trees would probably receive better care. And if problems did begin, they could be recognized at an earlier stage when effective treatments could be started.

LEAVES AND NEEDLES

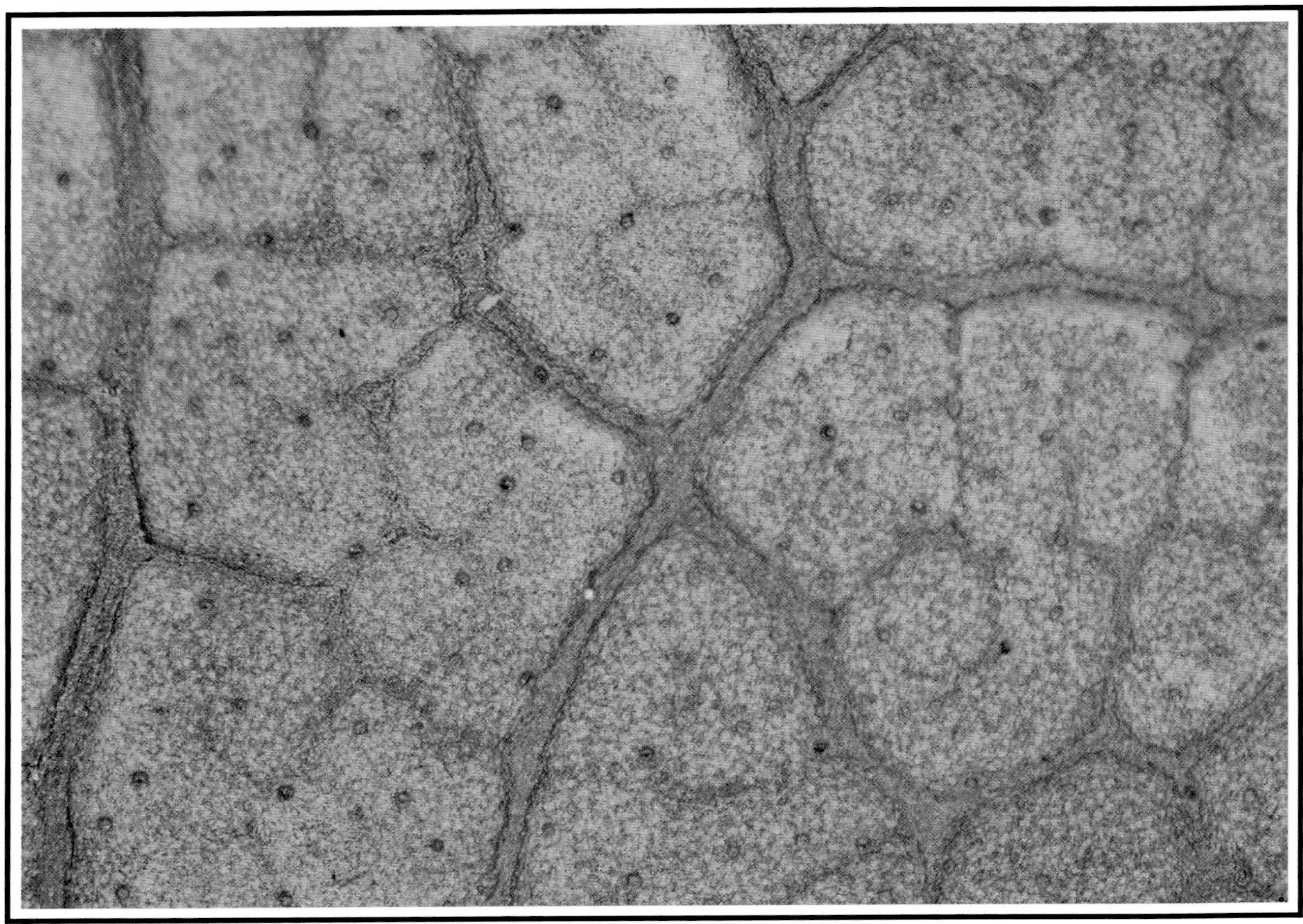

Mango, *Mangifera indica*
Young leaf with more red pigments than green chlorophyll.

Right. Red oak, *Quercus rubra*
Old leaf with no green chlorophyll.

Leaves are organs uniquely constructed for trapping the energy from the sun. As young leaves begin to grow they use stored energy that was made by mature leaves the previous growth period. As leaves grow and mature, chlorophyll is formed in the living cells. To form one molecule of chlorophyll, 54 carbon atoms connect with 4 nitrogen atoms, one central magnesium atom, and 72 hydrogen atoms. As chlorophyll is formed the first time, the elements must come from stored reserves.

NO ABSOLUTES
NO PERPETUAL MOTION SYSTEM

No system or machine will start itself and continue to operate or function without a continuing supply of energy. A tree starts life from energy stored in a seed. Or a tree can start from a cutting that contained stored energy. As the tree system reaches a rest period, energy must be stored to fuel the beginning of new growth at a later period.

TREE ANATOMY IS ABOUT THE

PARTS AND STRUCTURES OF THE TREE SYSTEM

AND THEIR HIGHLY ORDERED

CONNECTIONS.

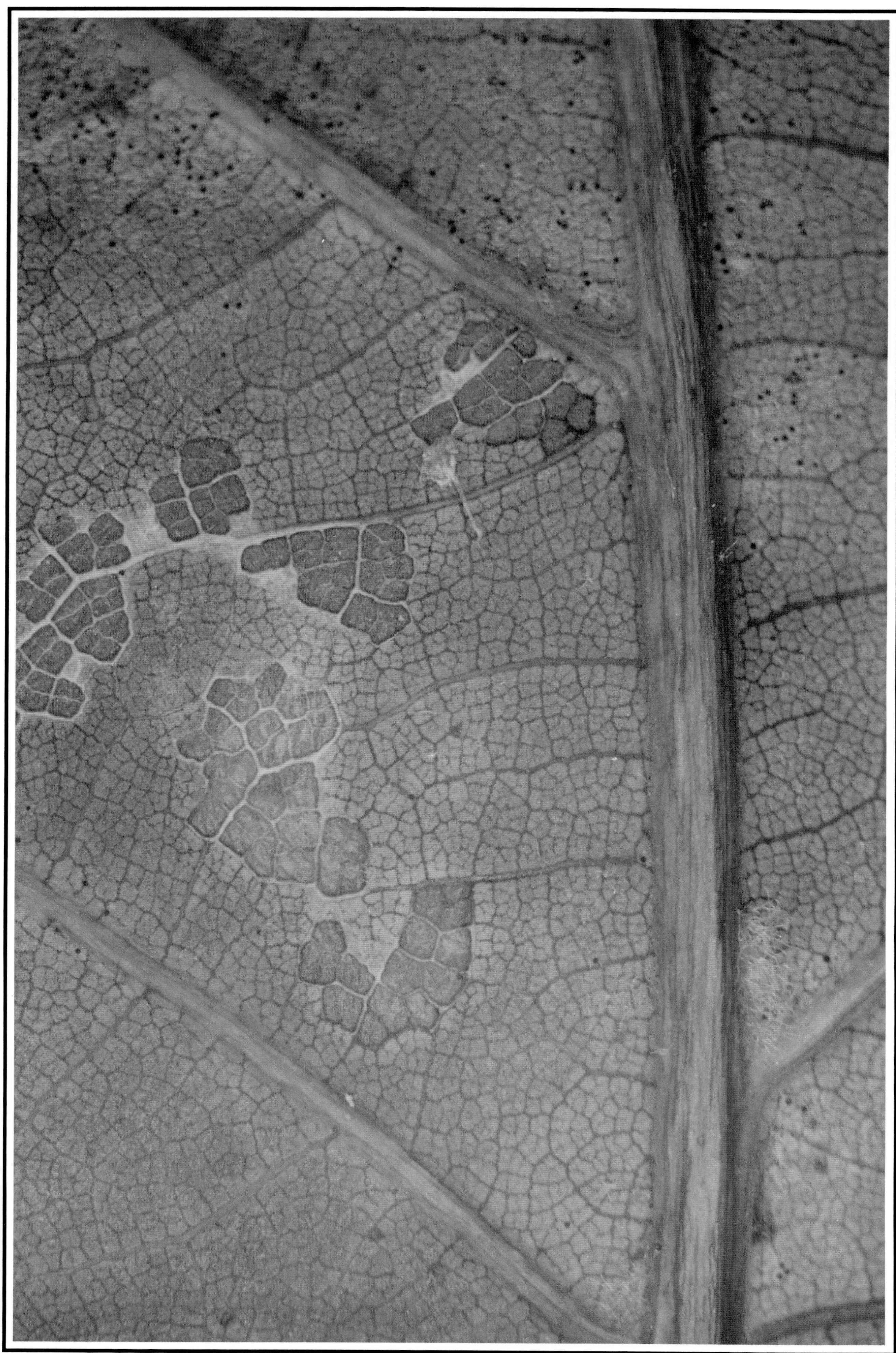

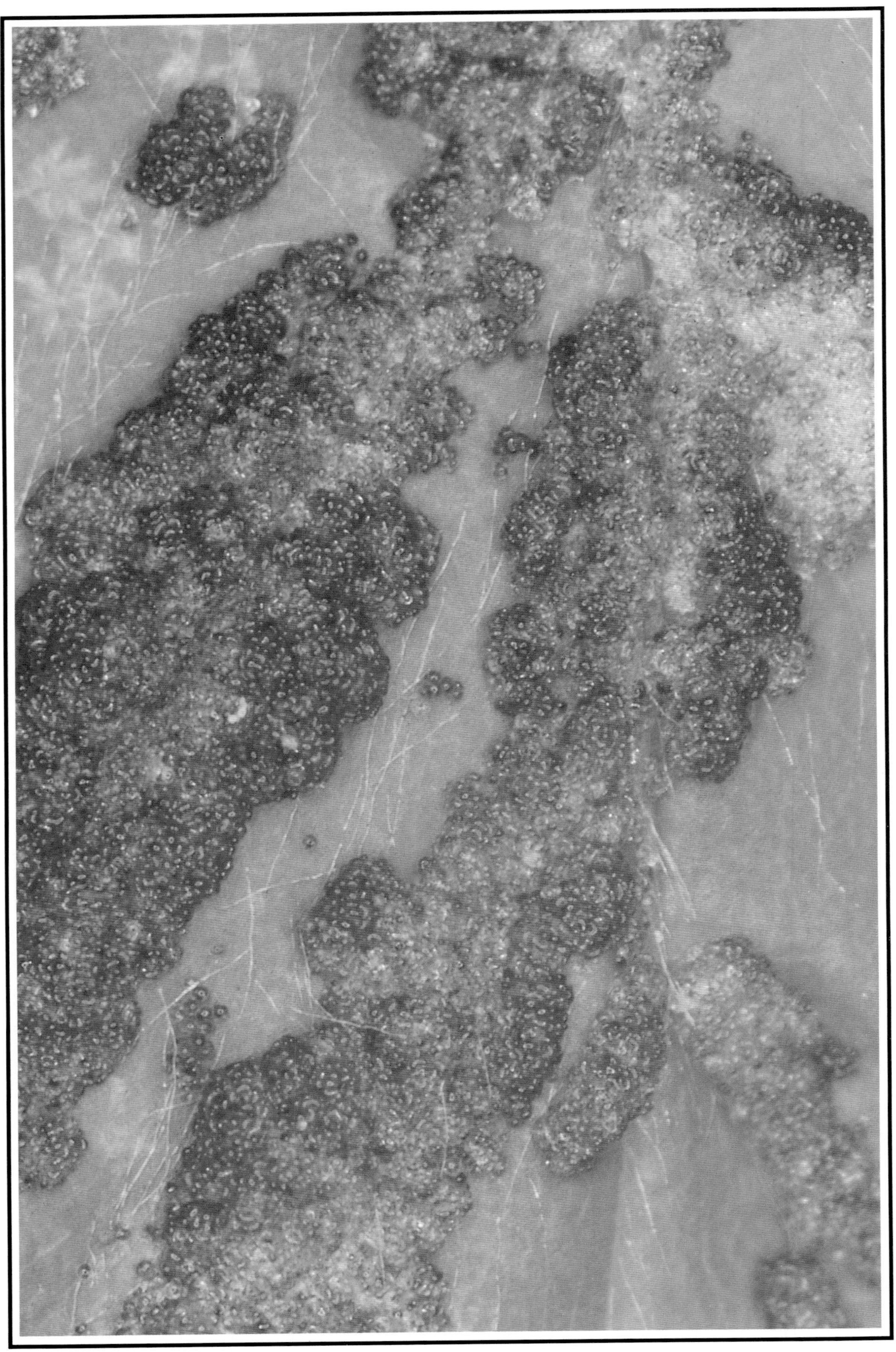

Sweet Birch, *Betula lenta*

Bright red, bead-like galls caused by eriophyid mites. Most mite infestations do not cause serious injuries to the tree, although the mite galls may kill some leaves. Many other organisms — fungi, bacteria, insects — infest and infect leaves. When leaves are seriously injured or eaten completely, the energy reserves and growth rate of the tree are greatly decreased. (See Page 44.)

Colorado Blue Spruce, *Picea pungens*

Needles are well constructed for extremes in temperature and moisture — thick waxy coating, sunken stomata, chlorophyll in shallow and deep cells. The angular shape of needles holds water droplets and collects droplets from fog. Fog water may be different from rain water because there may be more of the oxygen 18 isotope in fog water, and fog water can contain higher concentrations of acids and elements.

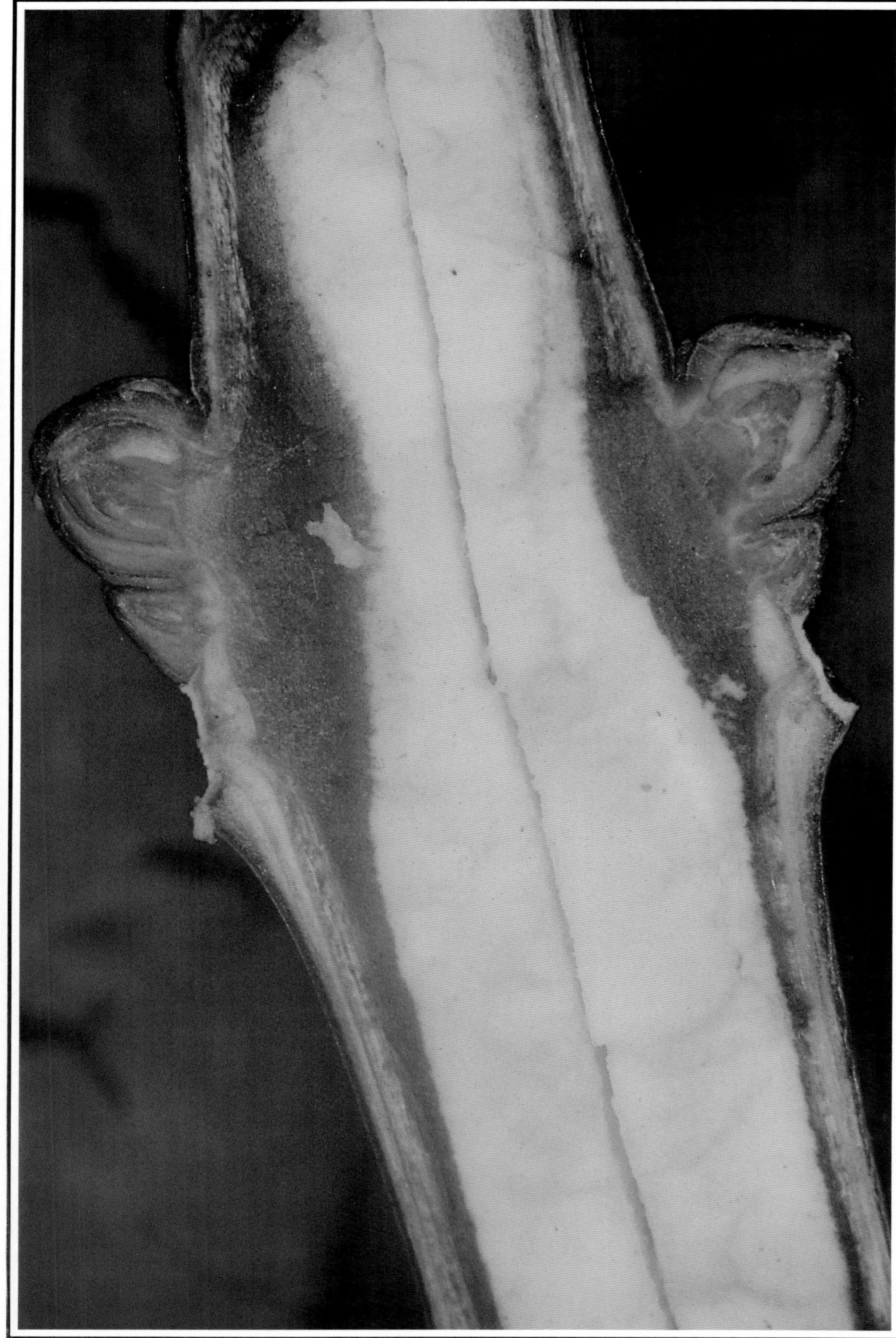

BUDS

Buds, Starch, Sugar, Pumps

The conversion of starch to sugar in early spring may so increase the osmotic pressure that bound water is freed and the turgor pressure plus the now available sugar could start the transport system.

American Ash, *Fraxinus americana*
Iodine staining of this fall dissection shows an abundance of starch behind each bud. Starch is not stored in the bud. No starch is seen in early spring.

Left. **Colorado Blue Spruce**, *Picea pungens*
Buds dissected in fall and stained with iodine in potassium iodide (I_2KI). Iodine stains starch purple to black. Starch is stored as an energy carbon source in living cells. Starch is not stored in the tip of the bud nor in the green meristem that will form the new growth the next growing season. No starch is seen in early spring dissections.

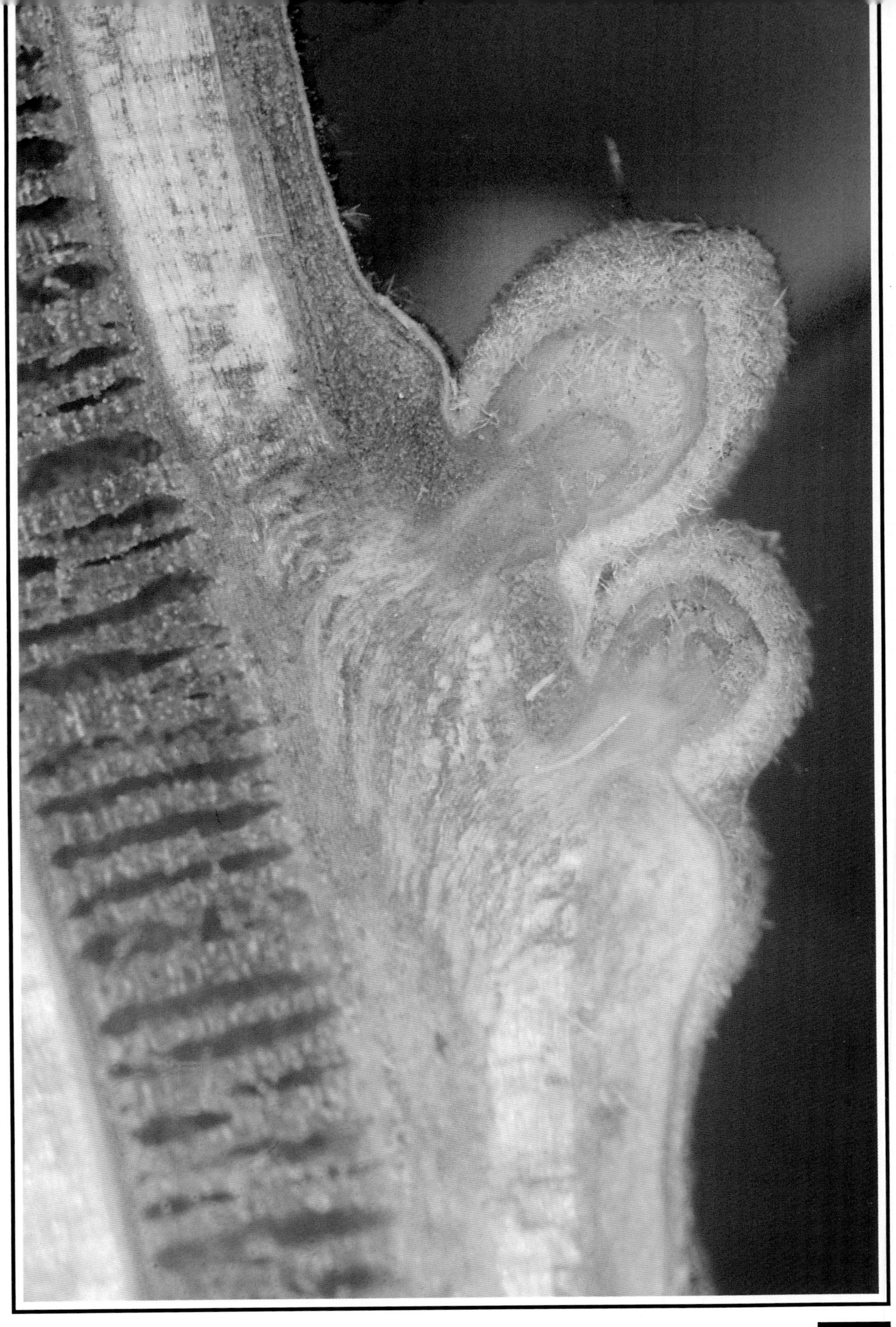

Black Walnut, *Juglans nigra*

Iodine staining shows the abundance of starch behind buds dissected in the fall. The chambered pith is a characteristic of the walnuts.

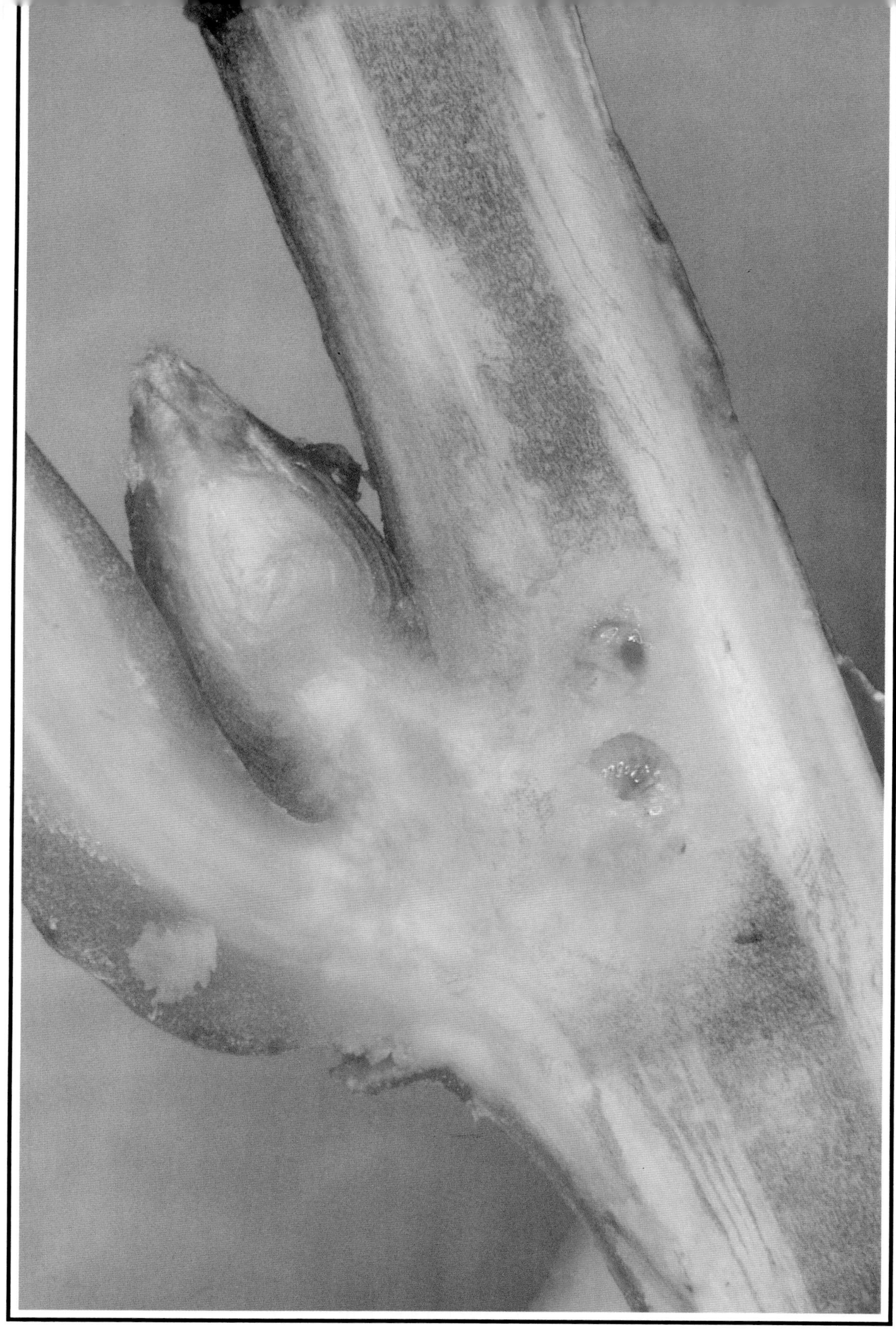

Red Oak, *Quercus rubra*
A fall dissection shows an insect larva behind the bud. Iodine staining indicates starch in the pith but no starch surrounding the insect. The insect has depleted a formerly energy-rich area.

Paper Birch, *Betula papyrifera*
A bud in winter in New Hampshire when temperatures were near 0° F, -18° C.
Many trees have ways of surviving in extremely cold climates.

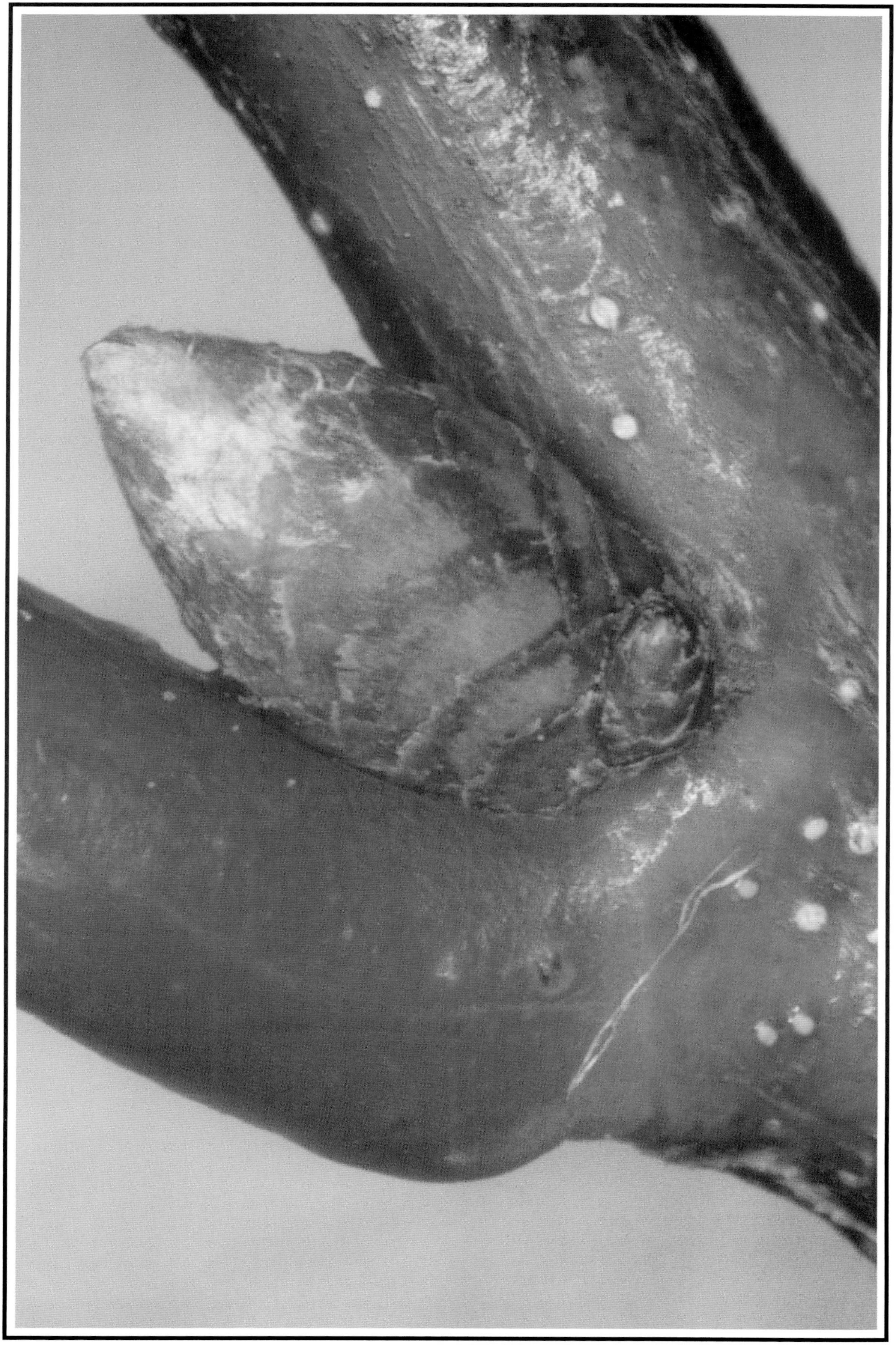

Red Oak, *Quercus rubra*

Late summer sample with the large dominant bud and the much smaller side bud. Seldom do the small side buds grow the next season. The small buds may grow when shoots from the large buds are injured or destroyed. Trees have many redundancy mechanisms that help to ensure survival.

PITH

American Elm, *Ulmus americana*

Hard tissues (lower arrow) separate the pith of the branch from the pith of the stem. (Review sections on buds to see that the buds are positioned away from the pith of the stem.) The upper arrow shows where the stem and branch tissues meet to form the branch bark ridge. When the beetles that carry the fungus that causes Dutch elm disease attack, they destroy the tissues in this zone. This type of wound gives the fungus easy access to the stem and branch. The sample was stained with iodine, and the dark stain shows the pattern of starch and of living cells.

Eastern White Pine, *Pinus strobus*

Dissection of a current year twig shows the abundance of chlorophyll in the pith and cortex. The current year growth on most trees is similar to an annual plant. There is an abundance of living cells with chlorophyll.

Red Maple, *Acer rubrum*

A one-year-old twig at left and the new growth from the tip of the twig is at the right. When new growth starts, the diameter of the new stem is usually the same diameter, or sometimes larger, than the stem that is producing it. The new tissues are very soft and the pith in the center is usually very large. The pith acts as a stabilizing tissue for the new twigs. As the other stem tissues grow, the pith is squeezed to a smaller diameter as shown in the sample at left. Both samples were stained with iodine. The new growth at right had very little starch, while the stem at left had a moderate amount. Much of the starch in the one-year-old twig is converted to sugar and used as an energy source to produce the new growth. The new growth has a thin covering called an epidermis. The one-year-old stem is just beginning to form a tougher covering called a periderm, or outer bark.

Right. **California Black Oak,** *Quercus kelloggii*

Most oaks have a star-shaped pith. Oaks have many very large rays and a great variation of smaller rays. This is a ring-porous species. The vessels formed in the spring are very large and the vessels formed later are very small. It is easy to count the increments of growth in ring-porous species because one growth period starts with large vessels and goes to the beginning of the next group of large vessels.

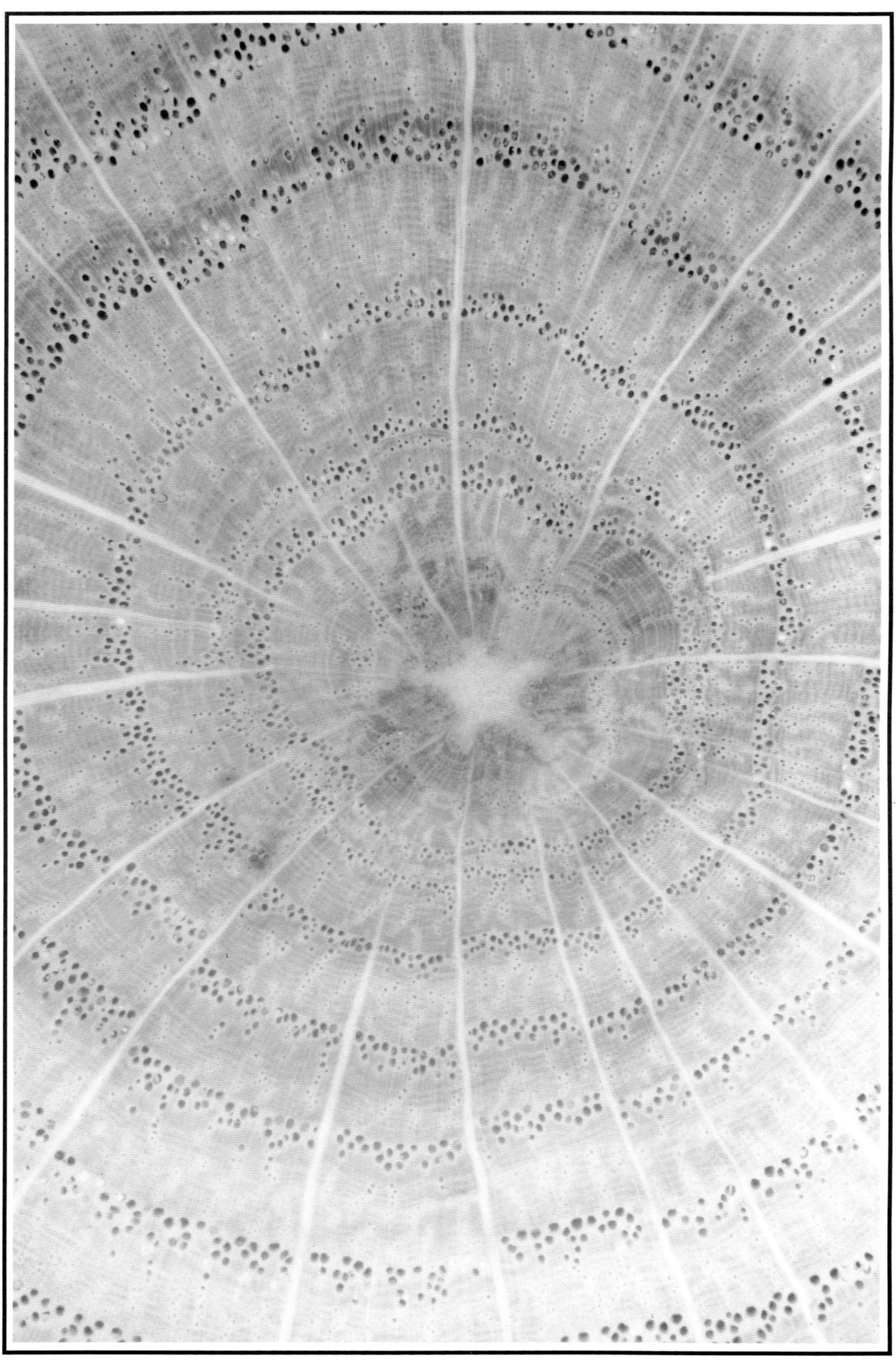

YOUNG STEMS

One growth increment

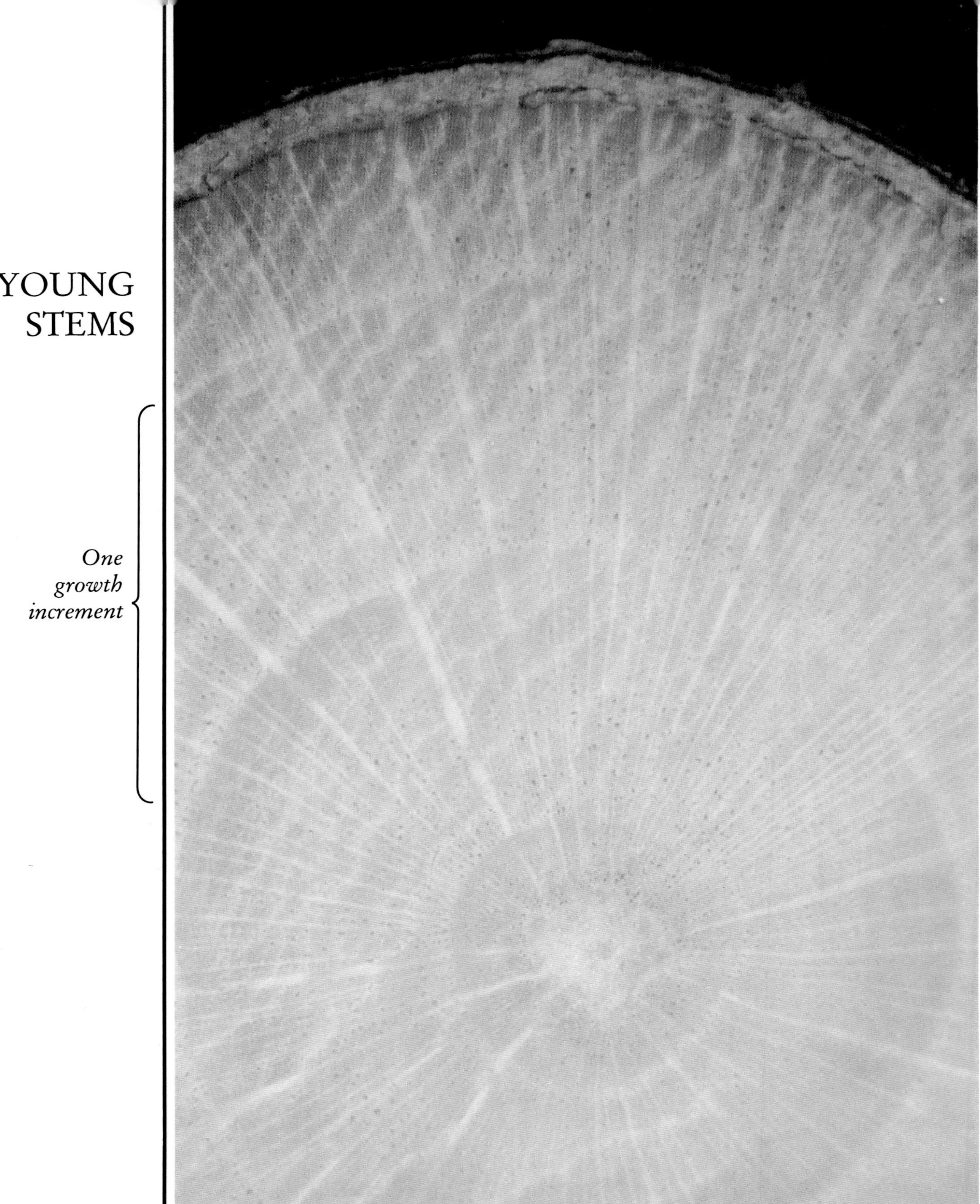

American Beech, *Fagus grandifolia*

The bright green color of young stems is common. The sample is not stained. Many trees have an abundance of chlorophyll in living cells in young tissues. This is a diffuse-porous species. The vessels are very small and scattered evenly throughout each yearly increment of growth. The rays vary greatly in size. It is difficult to count the growth increments in many diffuse-porous species.

Eastern White Pine, *Pinus strobus*

The bright orange bands of wood at the upper portion of the sample formed as the tree leaned in that direction. This type of wood is called compression wood. It is common in conifers that lean. Compression wood is formed on the downward side of the lean. In deciduous hardwood trees, tissues are strengthened on the upper side of a lean, and these tissues are called tension wood. Wood altered because of a lean — compression wood, tension wood — is called reaction wood. Conifers have tracheids, not vessels, that make up the bulk of the wood. The sample was not stained.

BARK

Paper Birch, *Betula papyrifera*
When the outer bark is peeled back, (center left) the green "cortex" is exposed. Most young trees have a soft inner layer of tissues that contain chlorophyll. (Whether it is correct or not to call this layer a cortex is a matter of interpretation because a cortex is supposed to be a primary tissue, or a tissue present only in the new growth.)

Right. **Small Leaf Linden,** *Tilia cordata*
The stained glass beauty of the inner bark, stained with toluidine blue.

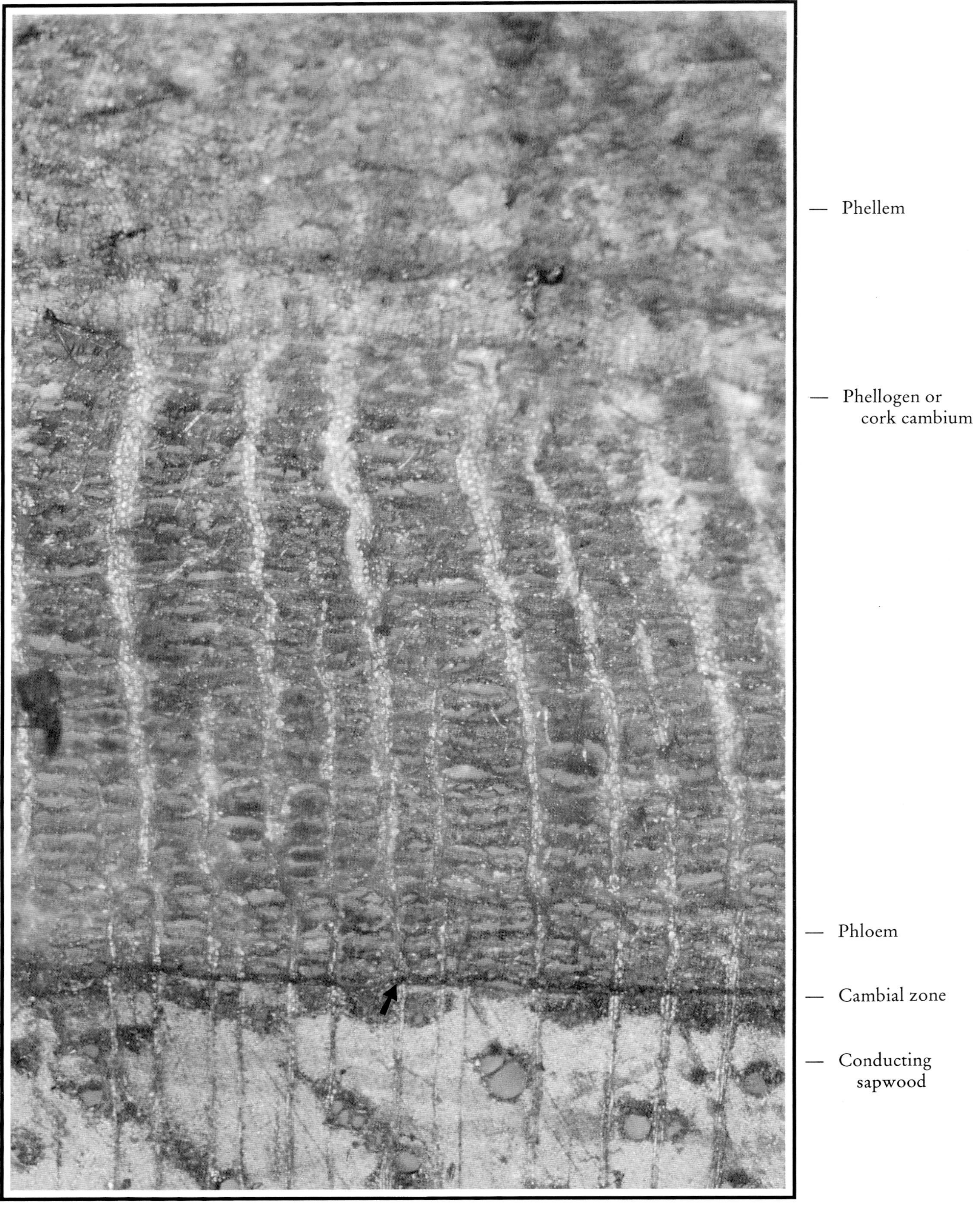

Black Locust, *Robinia pseudoacacia*

The wood rays expand as they continue into the phloem as phloem rays (arrow). Sample stained with toluidine blue.

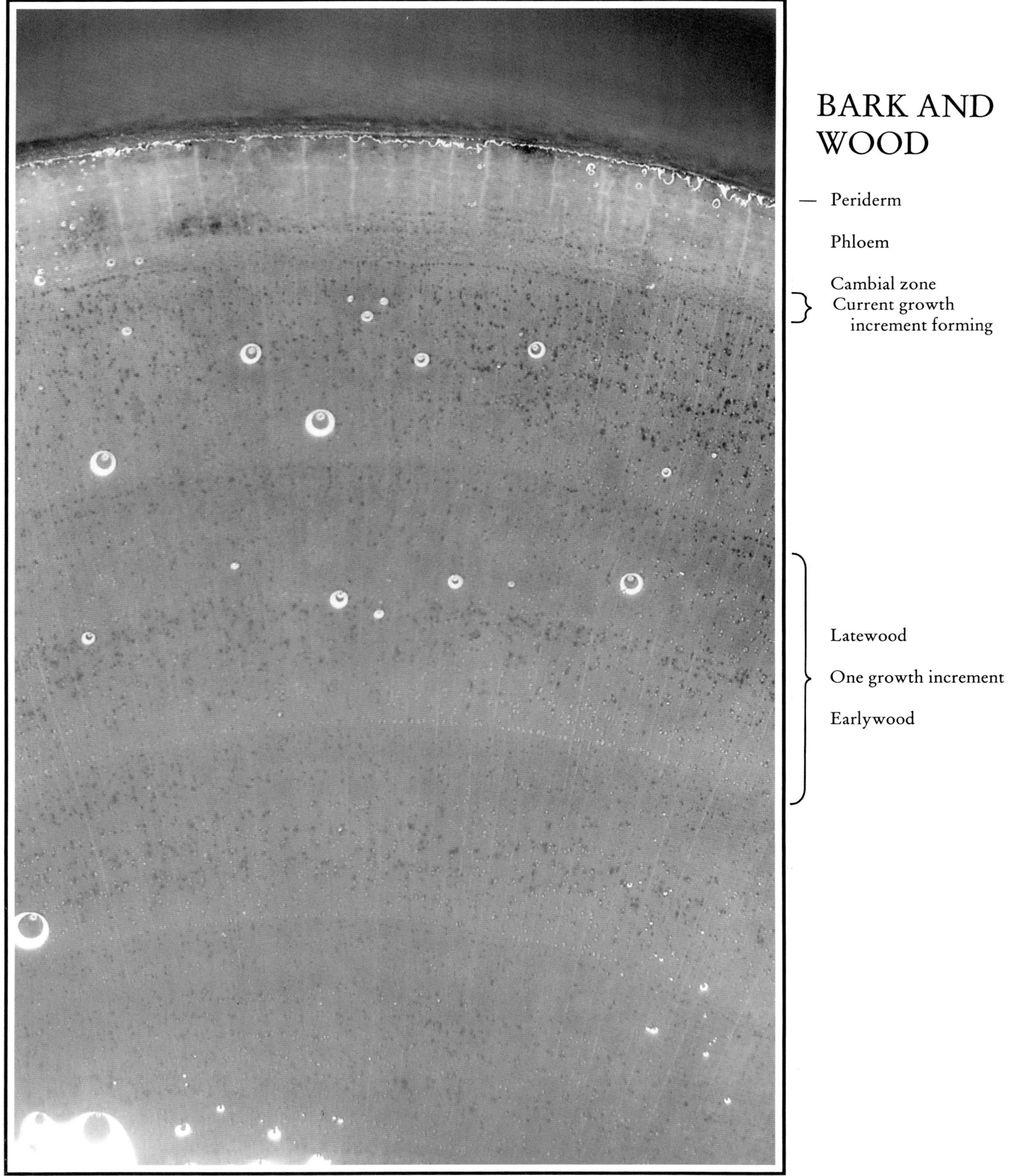

BARK AND WOOD

Madrone, *Arbutus menziesii*

The phloem contains a great amount of chlorophyll. The sample was photographed as it was flooded with toluidine blue stain. The clear circles are bubbles. Photographing under liquid was the best way to show the extremely small vessels. The early wood was stained more than the latewood. The wood is finely diffuse-porous.

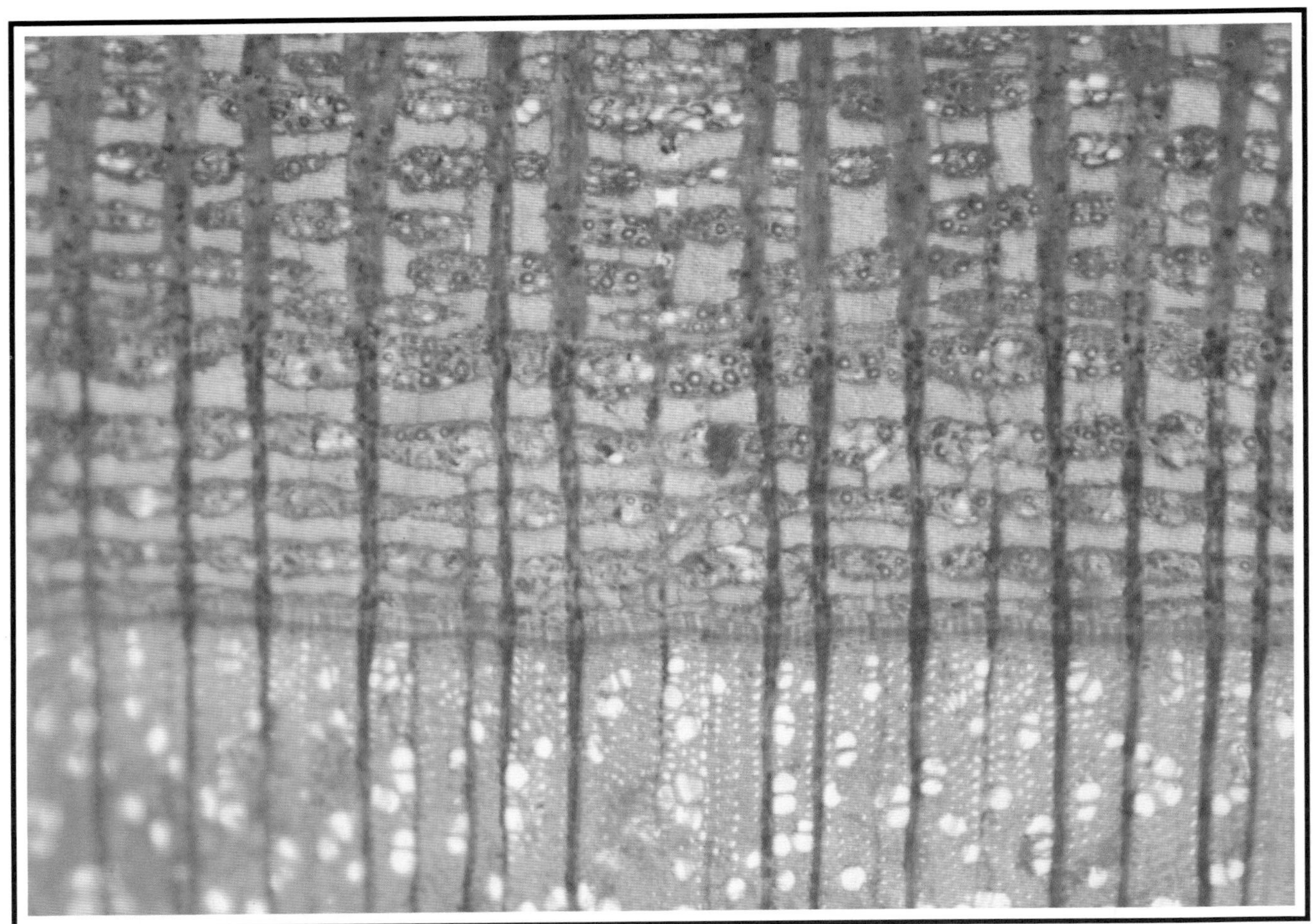

Tulip Tree, *Liriodendron tulipifera*

Wood and inner bark — phloem — stained with I_2KI. Starch was stored in wood and phloem rays. The wood is diffuse-porous and not very dense. CZ shows the cambial zone in the photograph.

Right. **American Elm,** *Ulmus americana*

The sample was prepared in late summer. It is not stained, nor was water added to the surface for photographic purposes. Note that free water was present only in the latewood of the current growth increment (CGI). Some tyloses were forming in the earlywood of the current growth increment. Tyloses plugged the vessels in the earlier growth increments. When water is discussed in trees, the type of water must be stated as either free water or bound water. All trees do transport free water, but how long they do it, and in which tissues is another matter. Many ring-porous trees transport free water only in the current growth increment or the one-year-old increment because the vessels deep in are plugged with balloon-like structures called tyloses. The free water then loads the cell walls and any small spaces between the cells. When the cell walls are saturated, that point is called the fiber-saturation point of the wood. Additional water then moves into the lumens or inner openings in the fibers. Because trees store water as bound water attached to the cellulose in cell walls, and as free water within dead fibers, the water stored may be as heavy, or more so, than the wood tissue that stores it.

Phloem is a transport tissue in vascular plants that conducts energy-containing substances from leaves toward roots.

Xylem is a transport tissue in vascular plants that conducts water, and substances dissolved in it, from roots toward leaves.

Wood is secondary xylem where some cell walls become thickened and heavily lignified.

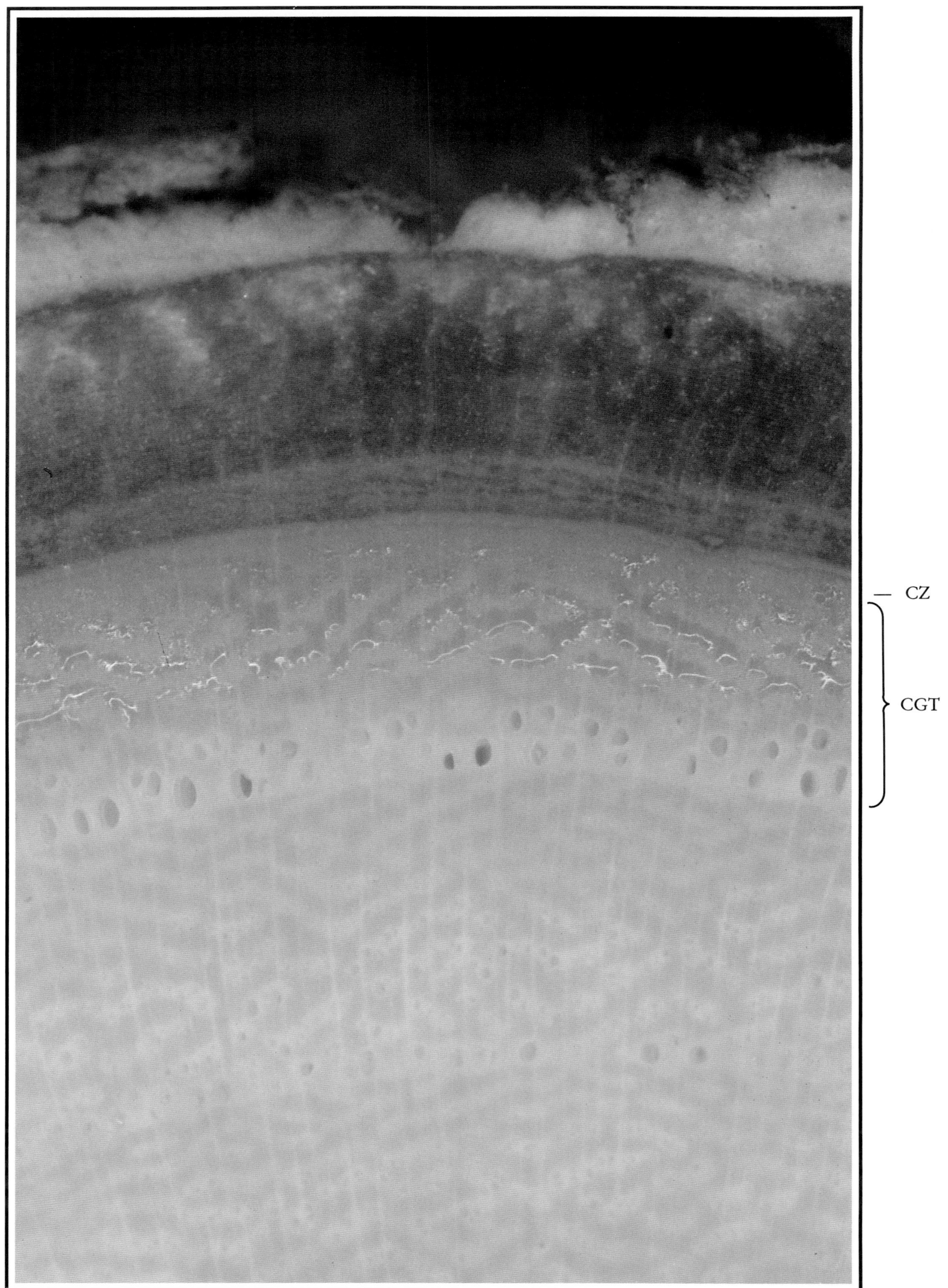
CZ
CGT

London Plane Tree, ***Platanus x acerifolia***

Chlorophyll is abundant in the inner bark of this sample from a young tree. The broad rays store an abundance of starch as shown by iodine staining of the sample. The wood is dense and finely diffuse-porous. The small vessels can be seen when a very close look is given to the photograph. The position of the current growth increment (CGI) is shown at right of the photograph, along with the cambial zone (CZ). London plane trees, and other species of *Platanus* shed their outer bark every year, thus exposing an inner cortex-like tissue that contains chlorophyll. Some smooth-barked *Eucalyptus* species have a similar mechanism for exposing inner tissues that have an abundance of chlorophyll. London plane tree is a major species planted in the cities of the world that are in a temperate to Mediterranean climate. The trees receive more injurious treatments than any other city tree, and most trees forgive and continue to grow. I believe they are so tough and forgiving because they store an abundance of starch deep into their wood and they shed their outer bark to expose the layer of chlorophyll-containing cells on their branches and trunk. Many tropical trees such as species of *Albizia* maintain a thick layer of cells on the branches and trunk that contain chlorophyll. And some species have long roots that "run" on land for great distances. The upper portion of these roots often have cells that contain chlorophyll.

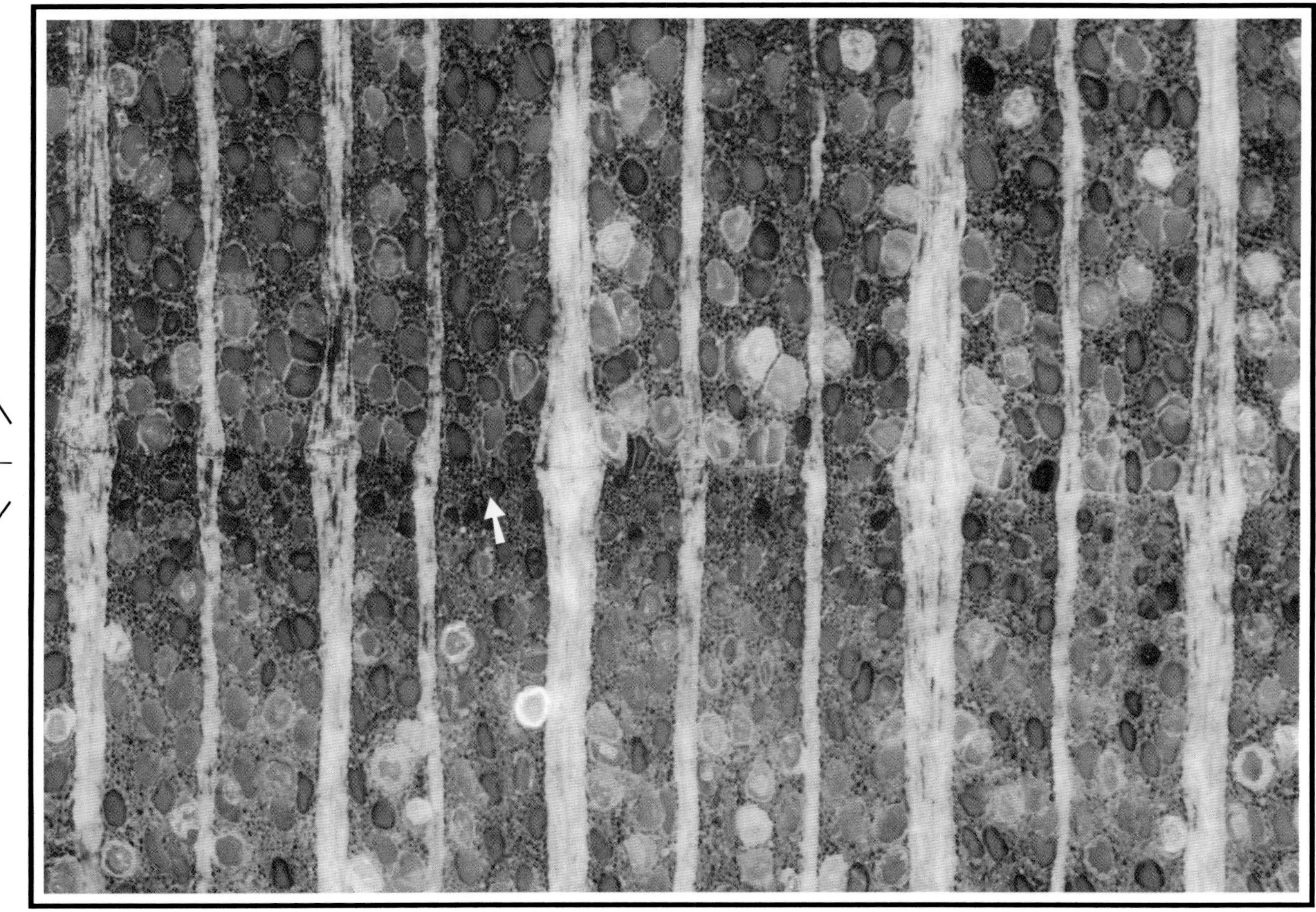

Petrified Wood

This sample of petrified wood appears very similar to wood of *Platanus* species. Compare closely this photograph with the one to the left — *Platanus x acerifolia.* The line and arrows to the left of the photograph above show where 2 growth increments meet. Note the swollen ray cells that are typical of the union of 2 growth increments. The cells at the end of the growth increment (arrow on photograph) are more compacted and are typical of cells called the terminal or marginal parenchyma. The sample came from California. It is always amazing to see that even after millions of years, trees have changed very little.

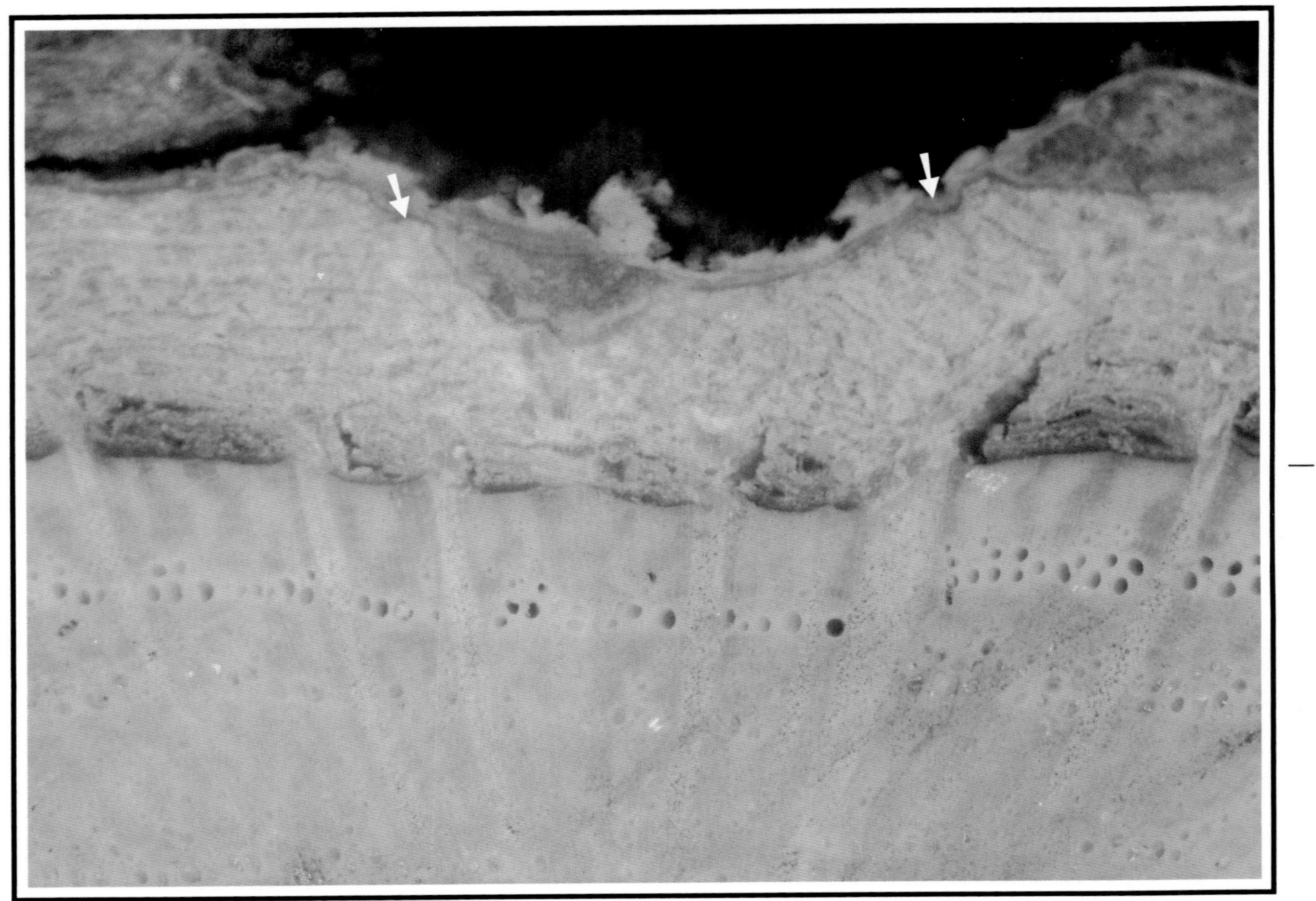

Oregon White Oak, *Quercus garryana*

The arrows show a layer of cells that contain chlorophyll in a bark fissure. Bark fissures are the indentations common on many thick-barked trees. The fissures meet the inner bark or phloem. Note the cluster of wood and phloem rays that are beneath the fissure. Iodine stained the starch purple in the rays. Only the current growth increment had open vessels. This feature is common with the white oak group. The cambial zone (CZ) is shown by a line at the right of the photograph.

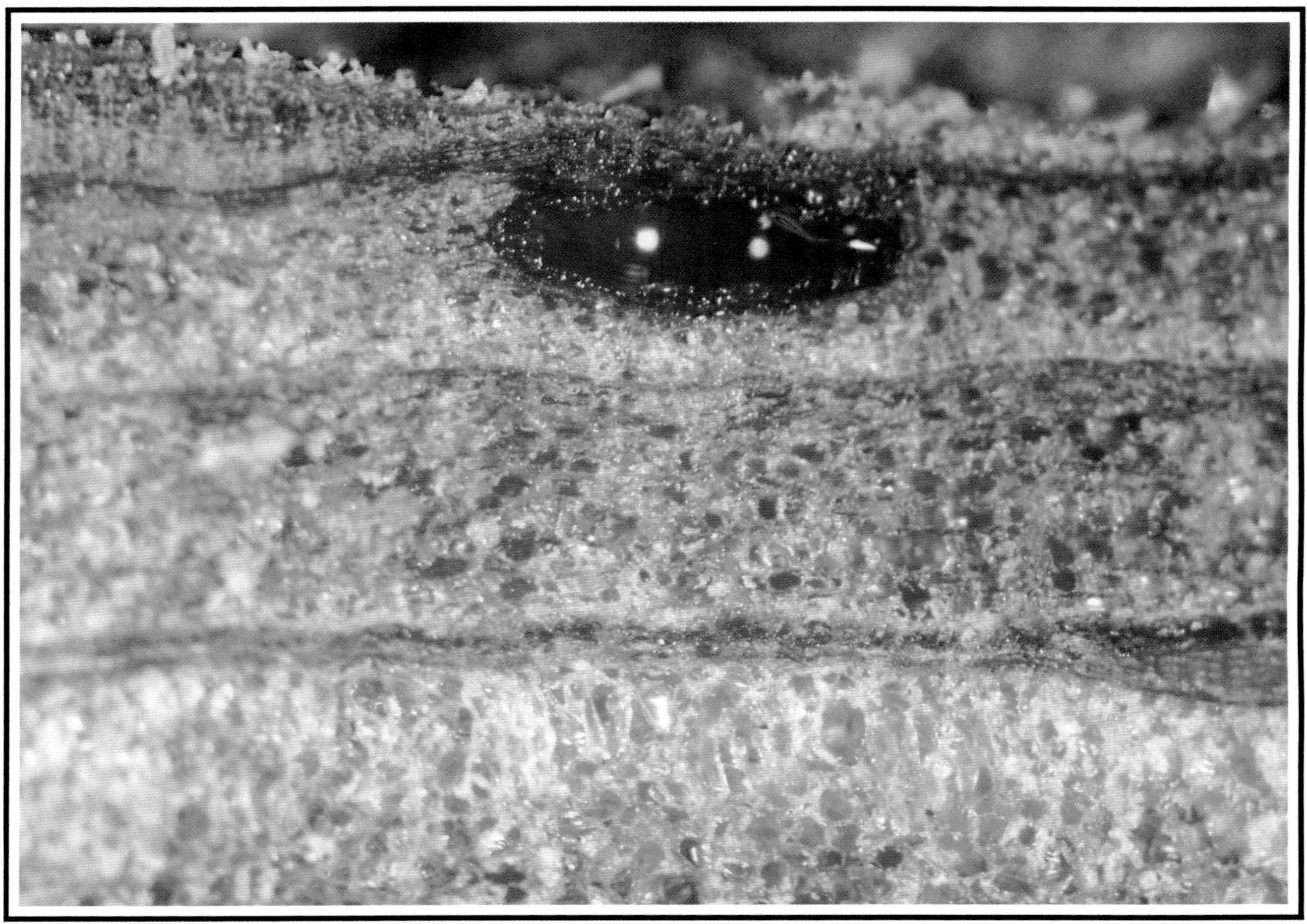

Gum Tree, ***Eucalyptus*** **sp.**

A small pocket of kino — gum — in the bark of a young eucalyptus tree. Most species of *Eucalyptus* produce a phenol-based material called kino in response to injury. The pockets or veins of gum are usually contained within the wood. Some species form the gum veins in the phloem. The phloem veins may be shed along with the outermost bark tissues — rhytidome. The veins in the wood often split out or rupture and the kino flows down the trunk. Kino veins in the phloem are found in species in the subgenus *Symphyomyrtus.* Xylem gum veins are common in species of the subgenera *Monocalyptus* and *Corymbia.* A few species of *Eucalyptus* produce oil glands in the phloem. Tannin-rich materials fill the glands. It is very important to remember that all of these substances come from carbohydrate reserves and form after injury. The amount of energy reserves in a tree is a major factor affecting survival after injury.

DUCT IN BARK

WOOD

Wood is a highly ordered arrangement of living, dying, and dead cells that have walls made up of cellulose, lignin, and hemicelluloses. Wood is secondary xylem.

There are two basic types of wood in living trees: sapwood and protection wood. Sapwood has living cells. Protection wood does not. Sapwood can range from two growth increments to over a hundred. There are two types of sapwood: conducting and non-conducting. There are four types of protection wood: heartwood, false heartwood, discolored wood in early stages, and wetwood.

Heartwood is age-altered wood. The wood is altered to a higher state of protection than the sapwood. Sapwood maintains an active defense system because of living cells. Defense is a dynamic process. Protection wood has many features that resist infection by decay-causing microorganisms. As cells age and die in some species, the cell walls and lumens are impregnated with substances that impart a protective feature to the wood. These substances are called extractives because they can be extracted from the wood by using various solvents. The heartwood is also more protective because it no longer has stored energy reserves, and the moisture content is low. Also , as the parenchyma cells die, nitrogen-based materials move out to the sapwood. Because of the low moisture content, lack of energy reserves and nitrogen-based substances, and the inclusion of extractives, the heartwood usually has a high resistance to microorganisms that cause decay.

False heartwood is wood altered to a higher protective state than sapwood as branches die and are shed. The wood in the trunk associated with the dead branches loses its energy reserves and nitrogen-based substances. The moisture content also decreases. False heartwood may or may not take on a change of color.

Discolored wood in early stages of development is a type of protection wood. Discolored wood is initiated by wounds and the death of branches and roots that are not effectively walled off. Bacteria and fungi that are not capable of decaying wood usually infect the wounds and the tissues associated with branches and roots that are not effectively walled off.

Wetwood is a type of protection wood similar to discolored wood in early stages, except that the infecting microorganisms are usually anaerobic bacteria. They also infect wounds, branch stubs and root stubs. The bacteria so alter the wood — high pH, high moisture, low oxygen — that infection by decay-causing fungi is stalled.

The great difficulty with this subject is that all gradations of all four types of protection wood may be in the same trunk. It is also possible to have discolored heartwood (normal heartwood that has later been discolored) and wetwood heartwood (normal heartwood that has later become wetwood).

The only way to understand these types of altered wood is to study them from longitudinal radial dissections. Central columns of "true" heartwood will be a uniform width throughout the trunk. Other types of altered wood will have an entry point such as wounds or branch stubs.

Great confusion has come to this subject because only cross sections of wood have been studied, and any type of wood darker than the sapwood has been called heartwood or a type of heartwood.

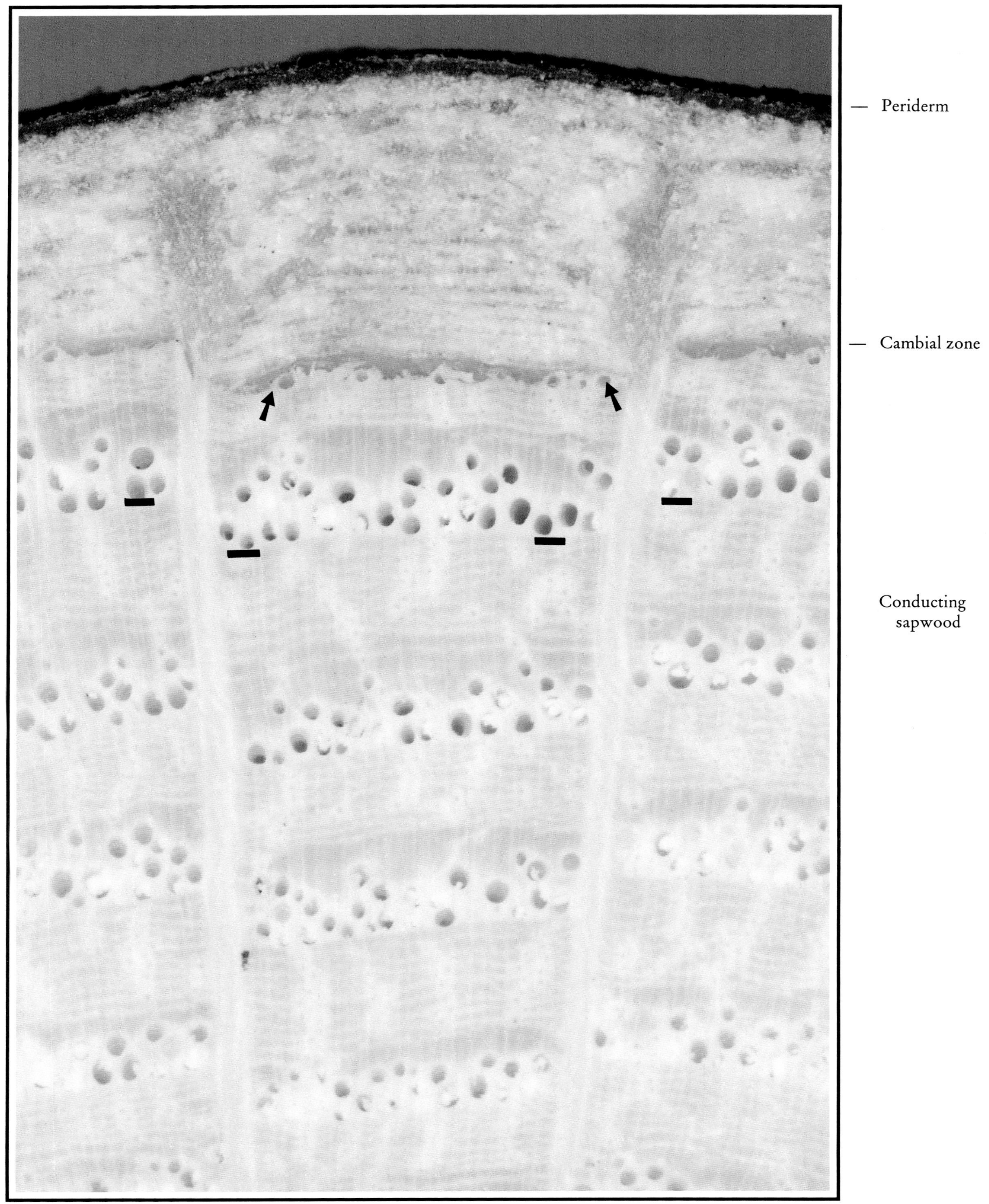

Right. **Red Oak,** *Quercus rubra*

A young sample of a red oak shows the first periderm and the green layer below it that contains chlorophyll. The arrows show the new growth increment just starting to form. The horizontal bars show that the increments of growth are not neatly circular. Each compartment is between large rays. The large vessels start the growth increment. Again, note that the growth increments are not neatly circumferential. This is more the rule than the exception in most ring-porous species.

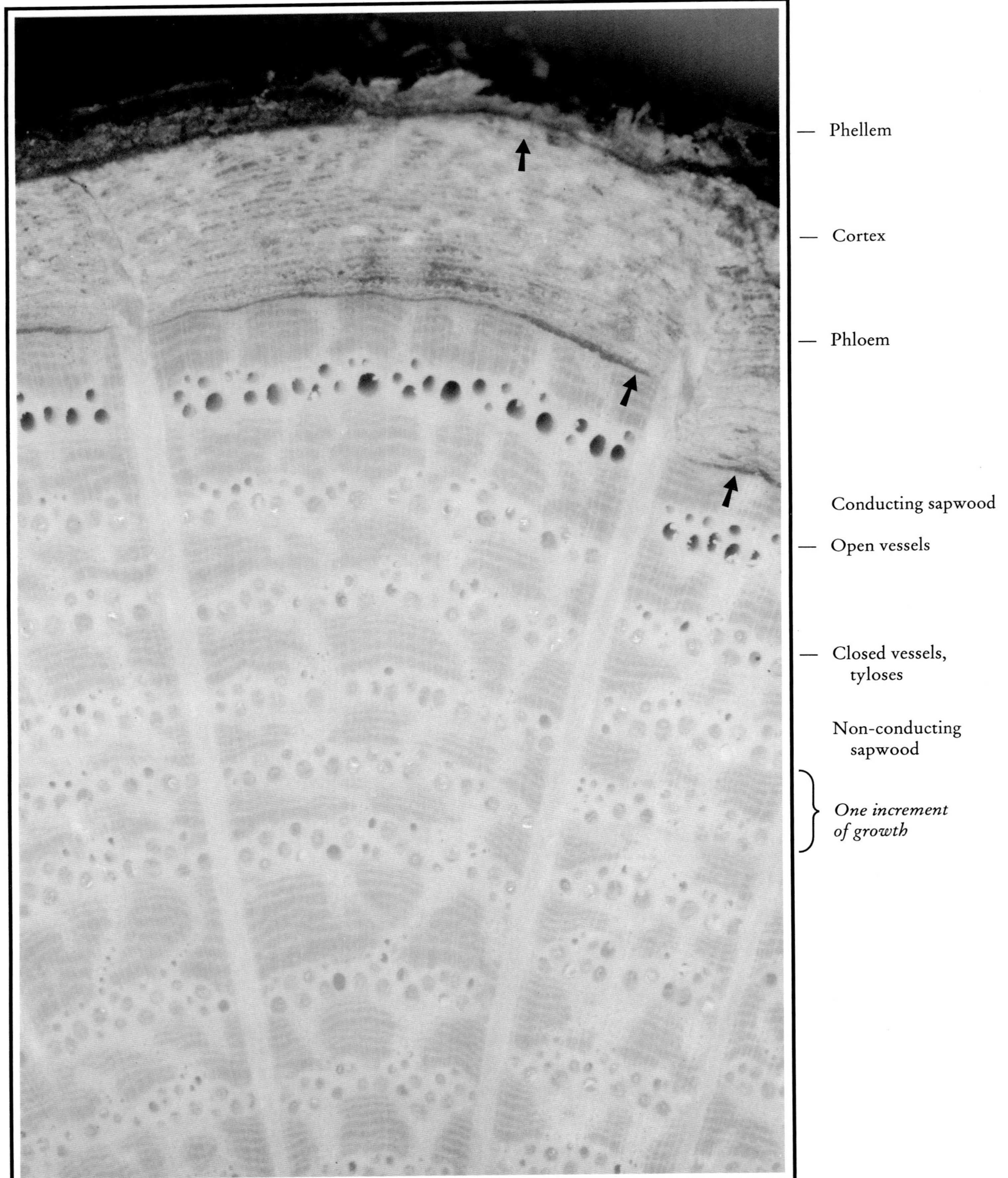

California White Oak, *Quercus lobata*

Most oaks in the white oak group have a similar anatomy. A common feature of the white oaks is open vessels in the current growth increment and all of the vessels inward plugged with tyloses. This is why species of white oaks are used for cooperage — whisky barrels. Oaks in the red oak group form tyloses only after injury and in heartwood. The arrow in the bark shows a patch of cells with chlorophyll. Note how the phloem rays fan out into the phloem. The lower arrows show again the offset growth increments.

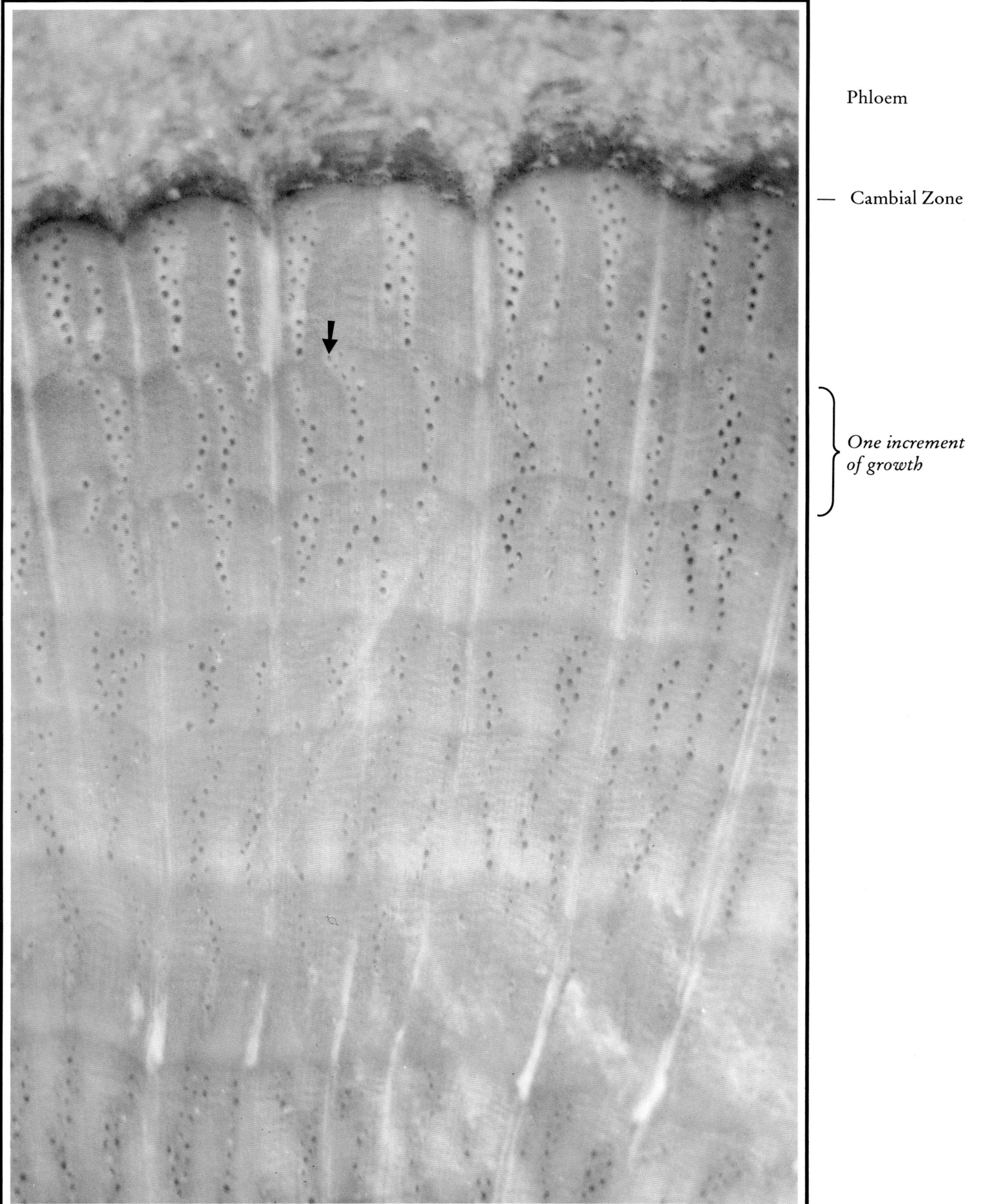

California Live Oak, *Quercus agrifolia*

The anatomy of the live oaks — *Quercus virginiana* in southeastern U.S.A. and related species — is very different from white oaks and red oaks, yet they are usually grouped with the white oaks. The growth increment in live oaks does not start with large vessels. The vessel pattern is more similar to those formed in latewood of other oaks. Growth increments can be discerned, but with difficulty. The arrow shows where the radial line of vessels ends in one growth increment. The wood in Tanoak, *Lithocarpus densiflorus* is similar to wood in live oaks.

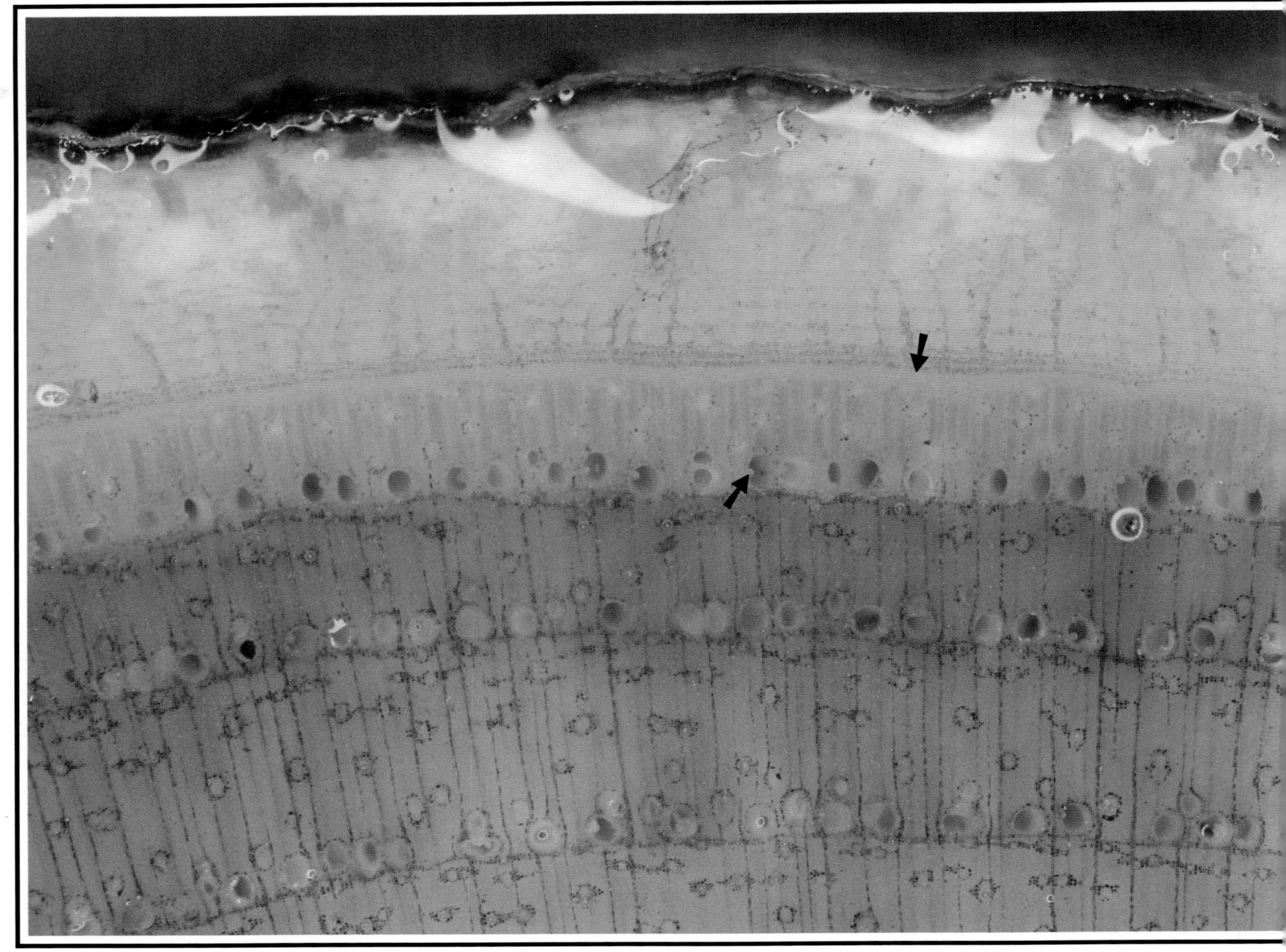

Oregon Ash, *Fraxinus latifolia*

This radially cut sample was photographed while flooded with iodine stain — I_2KI. The current growth increment was still developing and therefore it was using energy instead of storing it. Iodine stains starch purple to black, and very few dark starch spots are in the current increment. This is a common characteristic of developing growth increments in most trees.

The bark has a thick band of green tissues — chlorophyll-containing. Starch was stored in the youngest phloem. The upper arrow shows the cambial zone. It is free of starch. Meristems do not store energy reserves. They are supplied by energy reserves from other living cells nearby. The lower arrow shows a small tylosis just forming. The wood type of ash appears to be intermediate between ring-porous and diffuse-porous. Note that starch-containing cells surround each vessel.

Right. **Black Locust,** *Robinia pseudoacacia*

This radially cut sample was also photographed while flooded with iodine stain. The vertical arrow shows the axial parenchyma, and the horizontal arrow shows the radial parenchyma. Parenchyma cells have thin walls and an abundance of living material. Parenchyma cells usually do not have secondary walls. Parenchyma cells can live for over a hundred years in some trees such as the maples. However, most of the time they live for shorter periods of 3 to 20 years. Parenchyma cells do die in time. Starch is stored in parenchyma cells. The iodine stain not only indicates the presence of starch, but also the presence of living cells in wood and bark. All trees have a network of intertwining, axial and radial parenchyma. The network is similar to a 3-dimensional basket weave — the symplast. The symplast is the connected network of living cells in wood and bark.

WOOD IS NOT DEAD

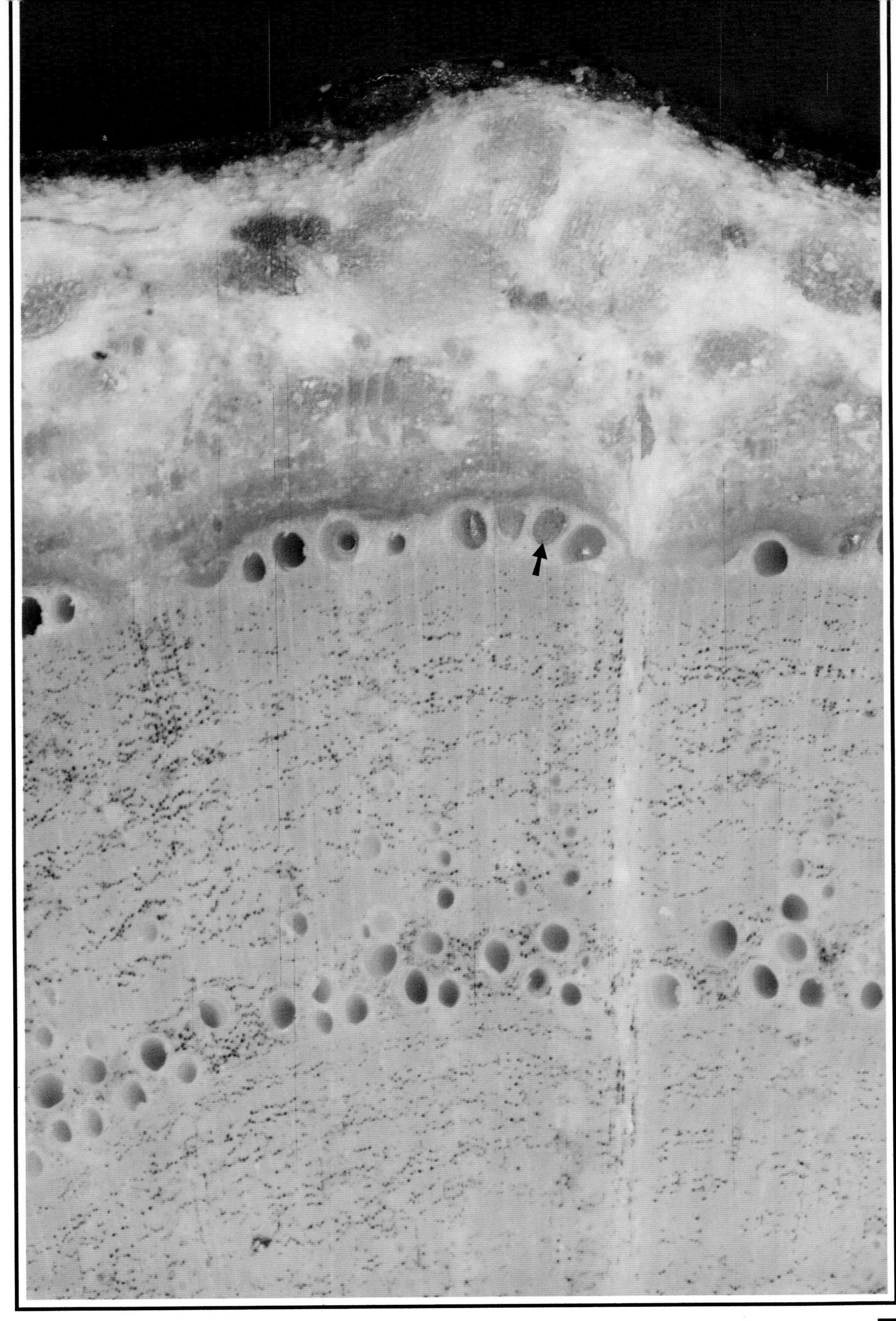

Red Oak, *Quercus rubra*

The new growth increment begins to form as the new leaves begin to grow. The first vessels that form still have the partitions between the cells (arrow). The vessels do not become functional until the partitions — septa — rupture and the group of vessel cells then form a tube. The sample was stained with iodine and the purple dots show living cells with starch.

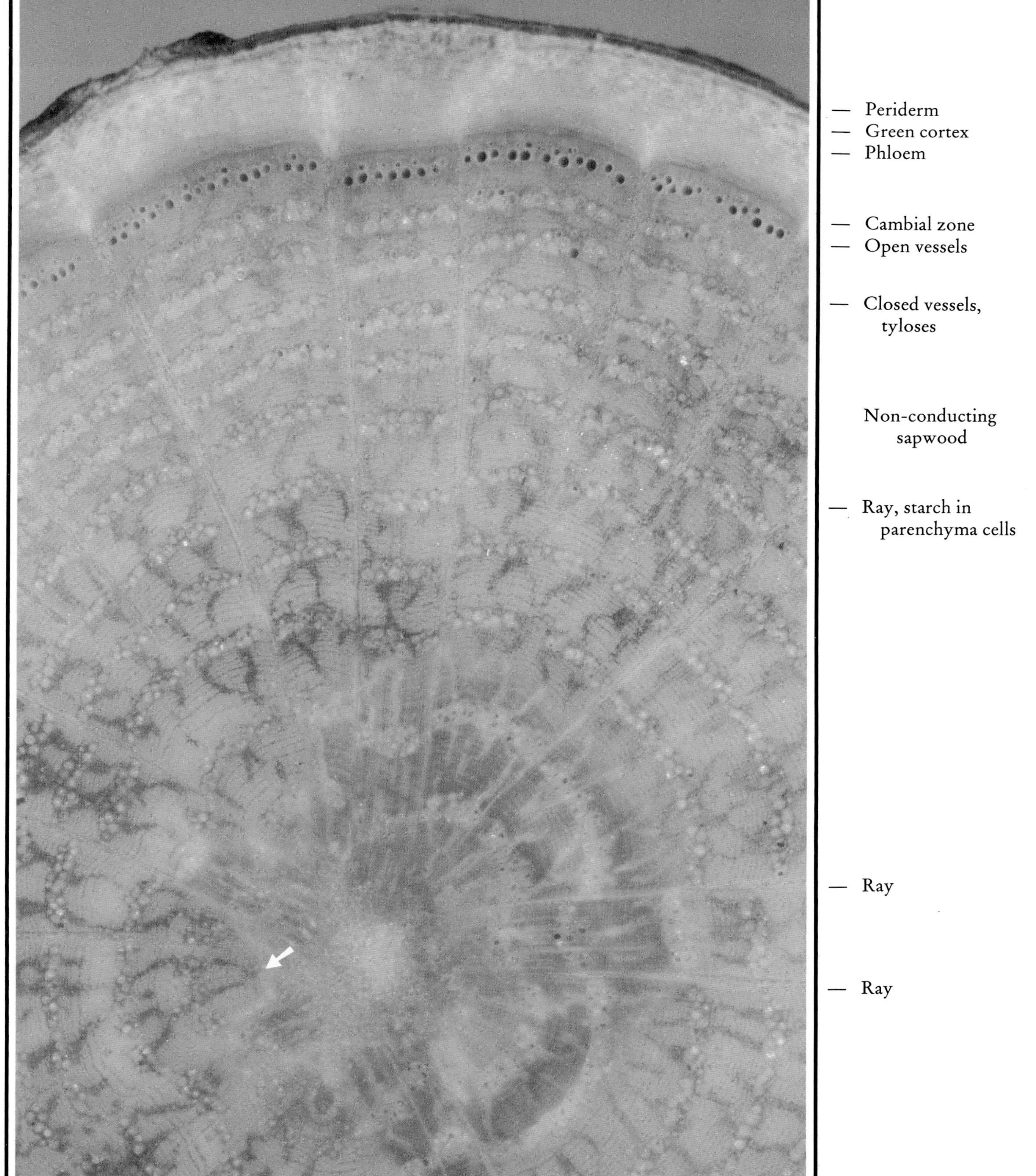

Bur Oak, *Quercus macrocarpa*

As with other white oaks, only the current growth increment has open, functioning vessels. Iodine staining shows living cells with starch into the center of the stem (arrow). (Can you see the star-shaped pith?) Two growth increments to the right of the pith do not have starch or living cells. These tissues are discolored and dead. They will not be altered later to form "normal" heartwood. Central columns of discolored wood often develop in heartwood-forming trees. The discolored wood is associated with wounds or poorly shed dead branches when the tree was very young. These altered tissues usually decay before "normal" heartwood does.

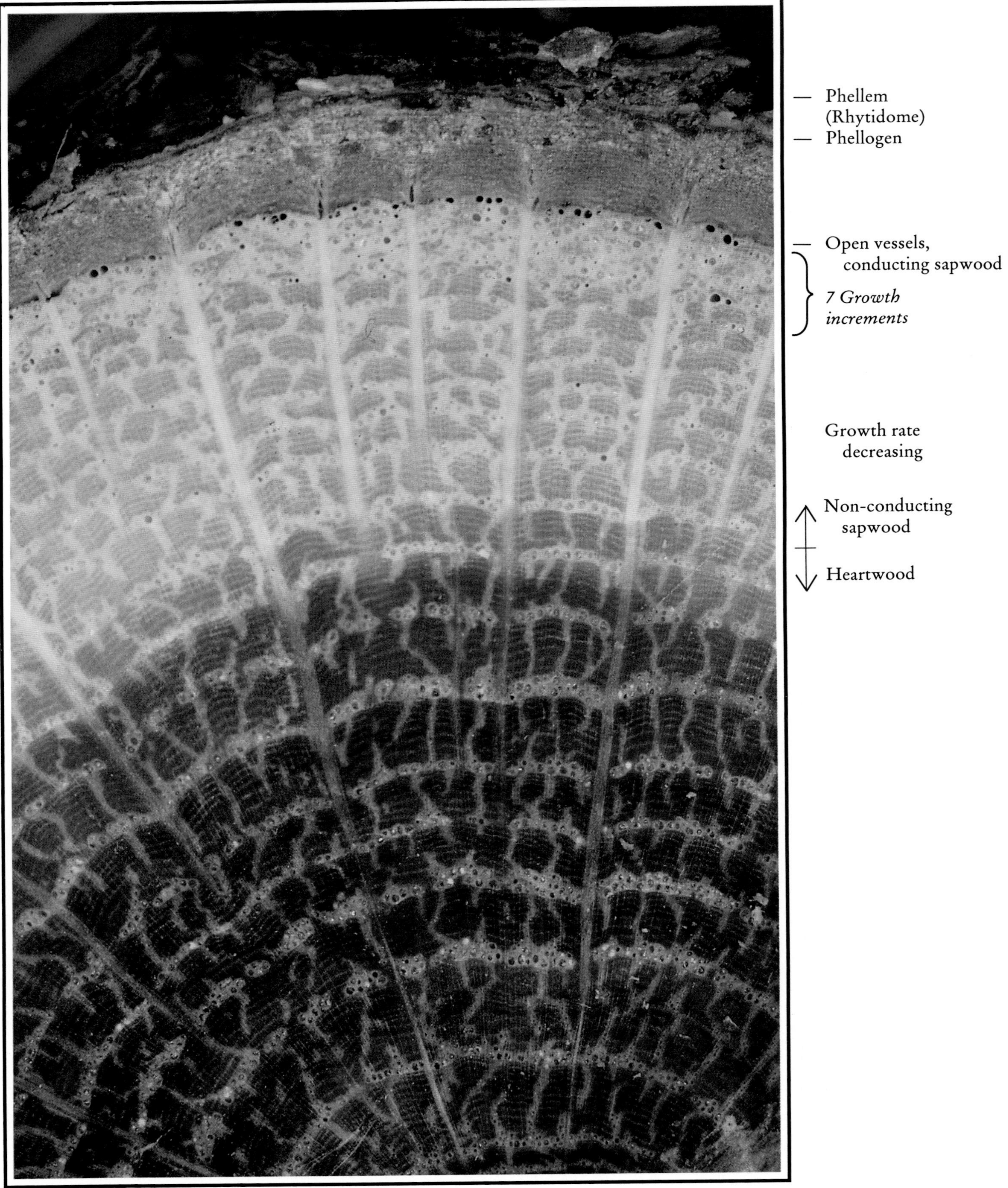

White Oak, *Quercus alba*

The growth rate of this tree was decreasing for the last 15 years. The last 7 growth increments consisted of only earlywood vessels. The tree was a victim of repeated attacks the last 7 years by gypsy moths, *Lymantria dispar*. (I was watching this tree for many years until it was cut for a housing development.)

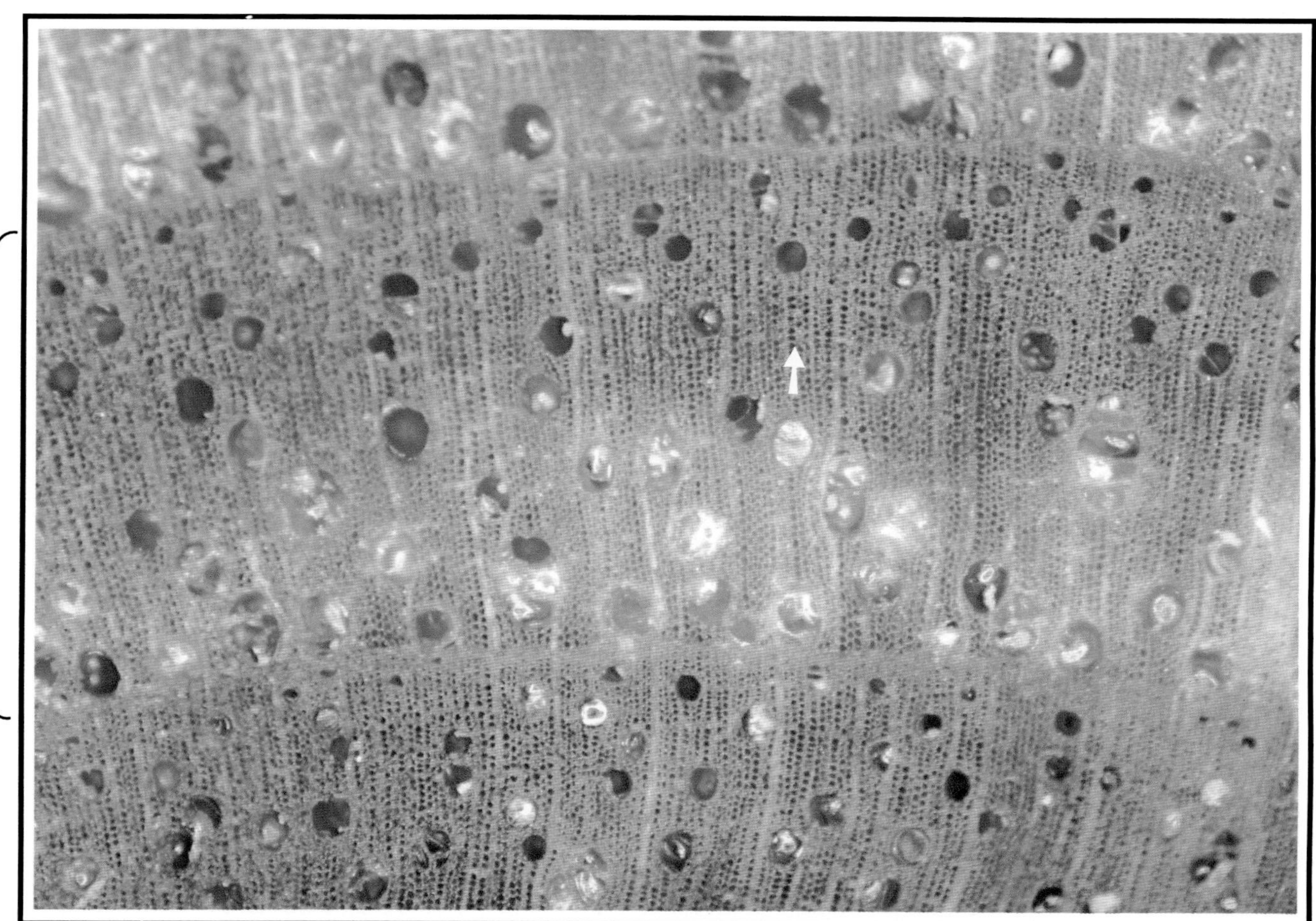

Black Walnut, *Juglans nigra*

The heartwood was stained with toluidine blue. The earlywood did not take the stain and the latewood did. The wood is more typically diffuse-porous or somewhat semi-ring-porous in some trees. Tyloses are abundant in heartwood. The wood is dense and the fibers are small and in highly ordered rows (arrow). These features of black walnut wood make it very shock resistant. The wood will also take on a very smooth satin luster when polished. These characteristics have made the wood very valuable for gun stocks, fine furniture, and wall paneling. (Heartwood usually contains less water than sapwood. The extractives occupy space that would contain water in sapwood. The following comments are applicable to heartwood, but much more to sapwood. I discuss the subject here because the photograph clearly shows the fibers.) Note the openings, or holes, or lumens in the fibers (arrow). When bound water saturates the walls of the cells, free water will fill the lumens of the fibers. Even though the water in the lumens is in a free state, it cannot flow out of the wood when the tree is cut because the lumen is surrounded by the cell wall. Maintaining high amounts of stored free and bound water is essential for the health of a tree. Wood that has a very high amount of water or a very low amount of water resists infection by microorganisms when wounds are inflicted. Microorganisms that infect wood in living trees have very exacting requirements for concentrations of water and oxygen, and for elements such as nitrogen, and for pH, and for temperature. Many trees live for hundreds of years and some for thousands of years with thousands of wounds because the "correct" combination of water, air, elements, pH and temperature that is required by microorganisms to decay wood is rarely present in trees. The marvel of wood in trees is its capacity to maintain concentrations of water, oxygen, elements, and pH that benefit long-term high quality survival for the trees and not for organisms that attack trees.

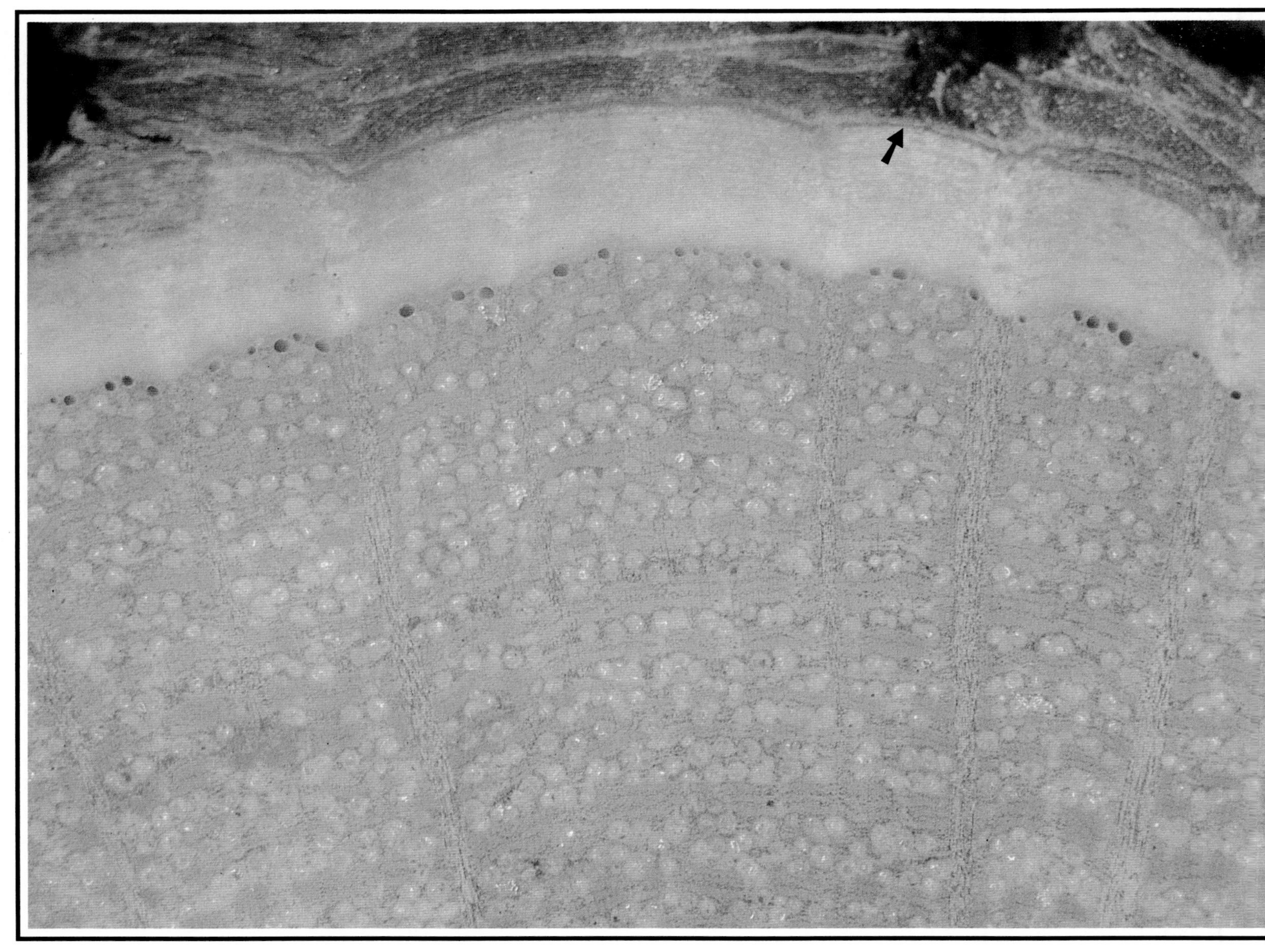

Gambel's Oak, *Quercus gambelii*

Gambel's oak is slow growing, compact, and usually grows in clusters. The sample shown here has approximately 20 growth increments. Iodine staining indicates living cells with starch deep into the 20th growth increment. The current growth increment consists of a thin band of very few open vessels. All vessels inward are plugged with tyloses. The question comes then, how are the living cells deep in the wood able to stay alive? I am not sure I have the answer. The few open vessels must load the wood with free water that is then bound to cell walls and stored free within the cell lumens. the connected rows of axial and radial parenchyma must actively transport substances essential for life. For such a slow growing tree an abundance of starch is stored. Maybe this is the key to how these trees survive so well in very dry, harsh climates. The bark is very thick. The arrow shows a green patch at the base of a fissure.

Trees that have the characteristics of Gambel's oaks would be perfect for cities. The trees grow naturally in clusters. They seldom grow tall. More clusters of trees should be planted in cities and parks. Where space is available, clusters have many advantages over trees planted in straight lines. Parking lots and malls are perfect places for clusters of trees. Small- maturing compact trees should be used when plantings must be done near electric utility lines.

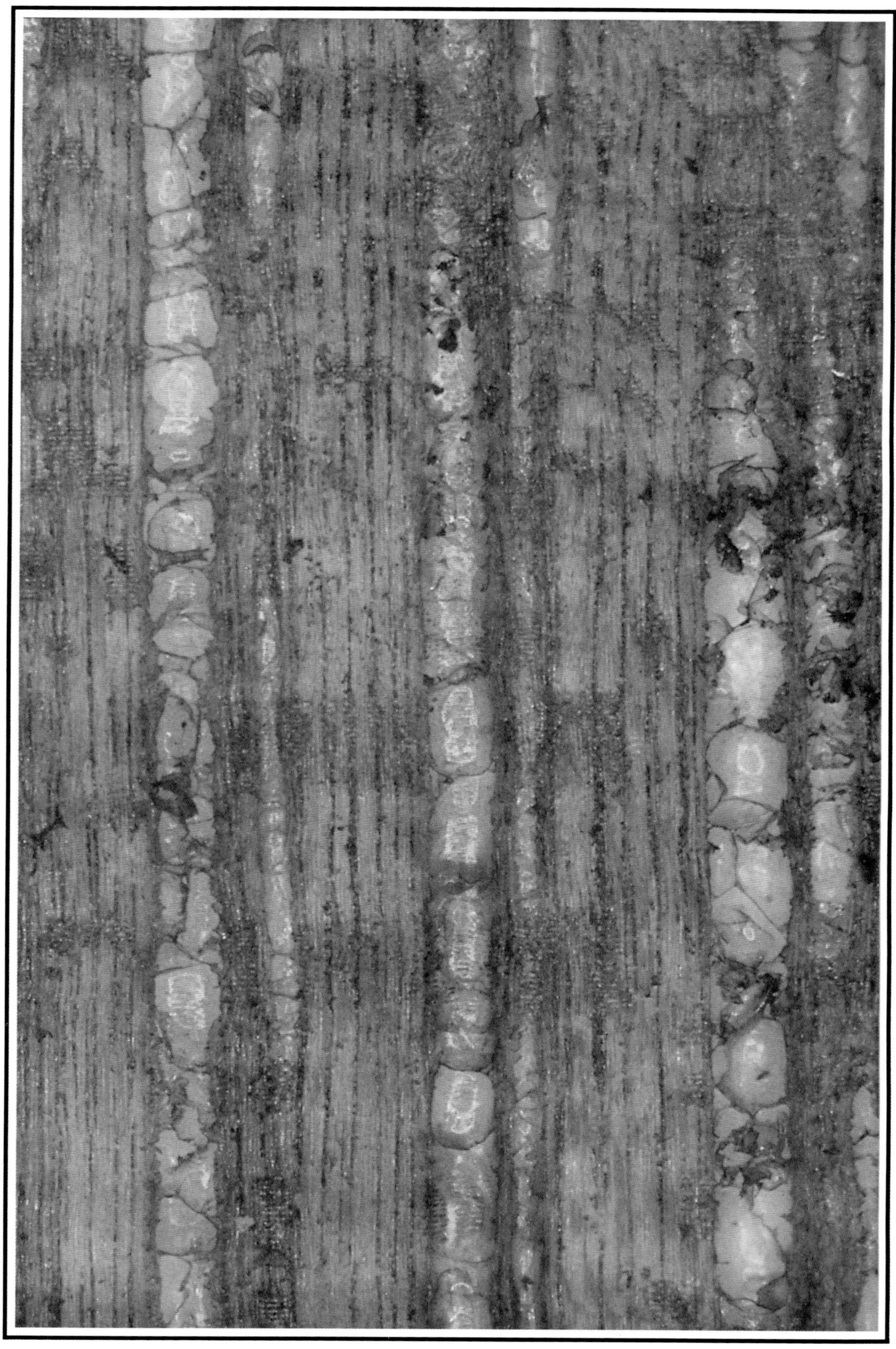

Gambel's Oak, *Quercus gambelii*

Staining with toluidine blue enhanced the beauty of the tightly packed tyloses in vessels in a sample of Gambel's oak. The tyloses appear as beautiful alabaster under the microscope. The tyloses are formed by the contents of the axial parenchyma that surround the vessels. Once formed they remain in place and prevent the flow of liquids in the vessels.

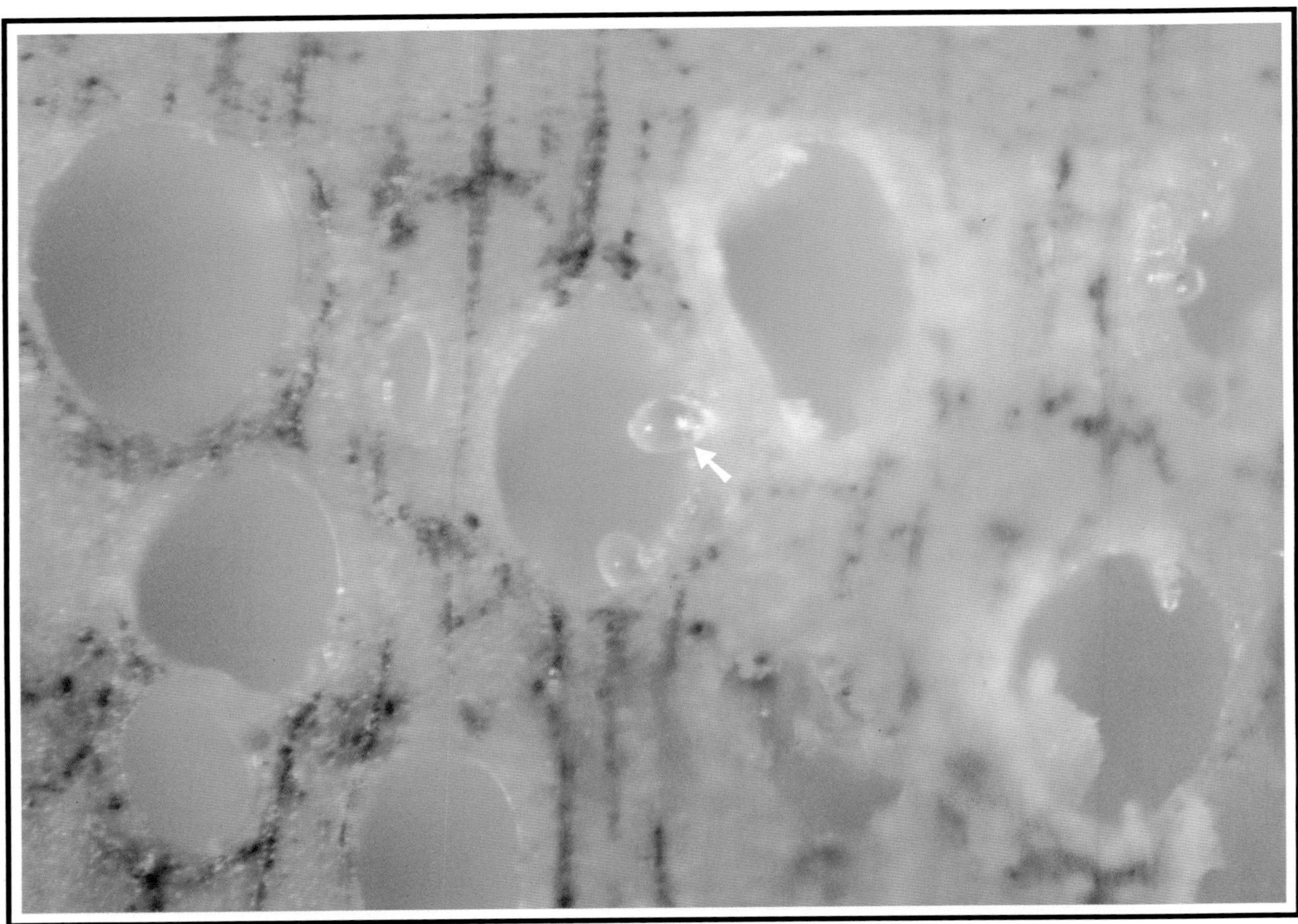

American Chestnut, *Castanea dentata*

The arrow shows a tylosis just forming in a vessel. Others can be seen forming in other vessels. American chestnut has only 2 to 3 growth increments of sapwood. Tyloses begin forming in the second increment. This means that American chestnut has one growth increment of conducting sapwood, and one or two increments of non-conducting sapwood. These features make chestnut a very durable wood. That is the beneficial part. The not-so-beneficial part is that the trees maintain a very small amount of energy reserves in the sapwood. *Castanea sativa*, which is much more resistant to chestnut blight, maintains several sapwood growth increments that store energy reserves.

Castanea dentata is very susceptible to *Cryphonectria parasitica* (syn. *Endothia parasitica*) that causes chestnut blight. The fungus infects and kills the bark. The disease has been studied intensely, but mostly from the view of the pathogen. Very little research has been done on the defense system, or lack of a defense system, of the tree. American chestnut differs from oaks in that chestnut has very narrow rays, and again small energy storage capacity.

American chestnut was a dominant species in the Appalachian forest of the U.S.A. The trees were very tall, very massive, and very long-lived. I believe they developed as trees that allocated most of their energy for growth and reproduction. They had few serious natural enemies. Their energy reserves for defense were very low in comparison to their great size. Then came the fungus. The giants fell rapidly. Many American chestnut trees still grow in forests in the eastern U.S.A., but most trees rarely grow over 5 meters tall before they are infected.

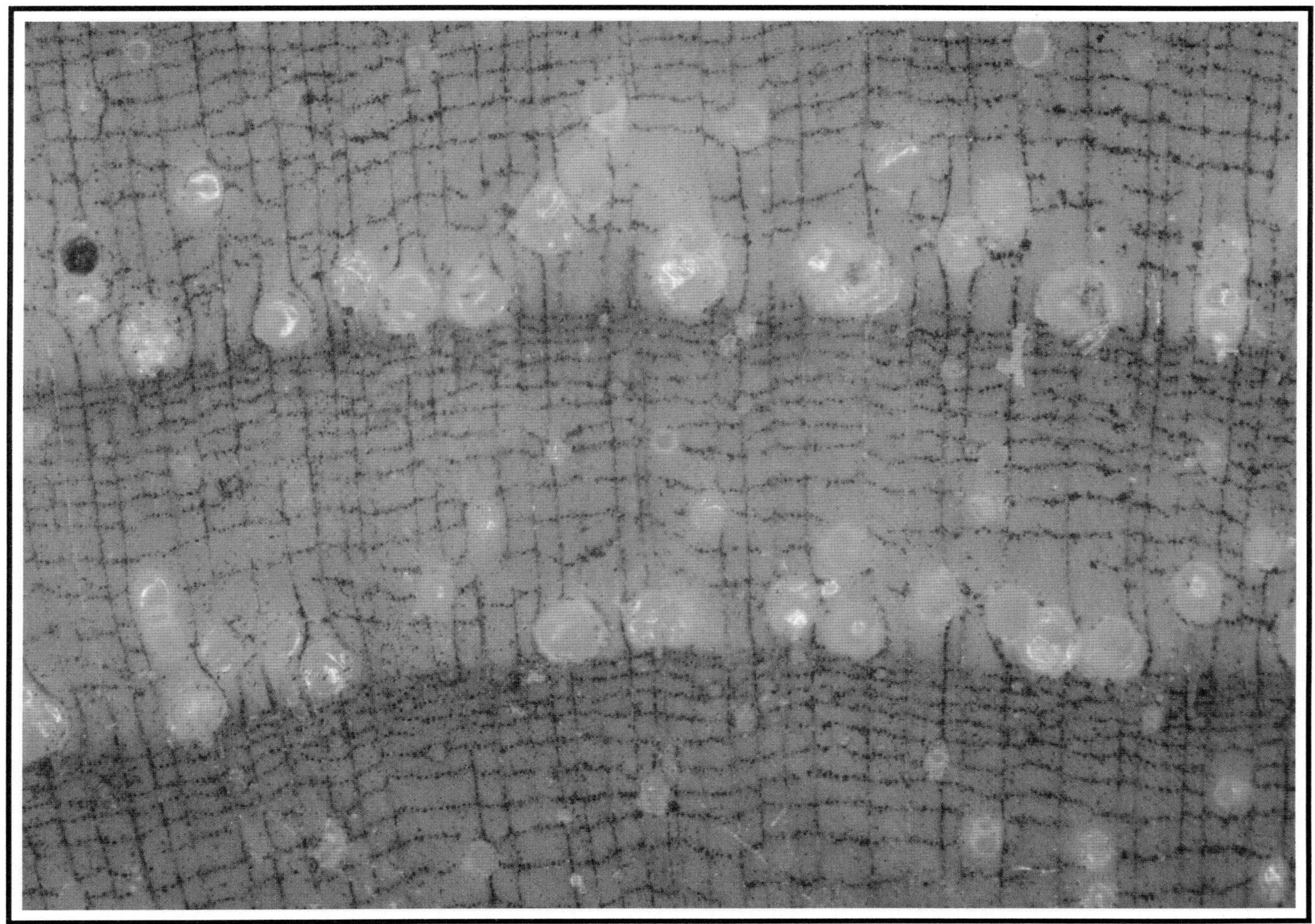

Sassafras, ***Sassafras albidum***

This iodine-stained sample shows clearly a portion of the symplast. The symplast is the living connected network of cells in a tree. The living axial and radial parenchyma make up the symplast in the wood. The living cells with iodine-stained starch granules in them form a perfect grid or block-type pattern. The vertical purple lines are formed by the radial parenchyma and the circumferential or horizontal lines are formed by the axial parenchyma. The living network of cells in the wood connects with the cambial zone, the living phloem rays and cork cambium or phellogen. Within the symplast lie the dead fibers and vessels, small spaces between some cells, and cell walls. All of these dead parts make up the apoplast. In a sense, there are two 3-dimensional basket-type networks. The symplast connects all the living parts and the apoplast makes up all the framework for the remaining parts. The apoplast is very important for water storage. The symplast is very important for energy storage, and for dynamic transport of substances. Note that in this sassafras sample, as in other samples shown in this book, that the symplast surrounds vessels that have tyloses. The point here is that tyloses alone are not features that define heartwood. The sample here shows non-conducting sapwood. Sapwood in trees contains a very great number of living cells. Wood is a highly ordered arrangement of living, dying, and dead cells. The myth that wood is dead must be corrected.

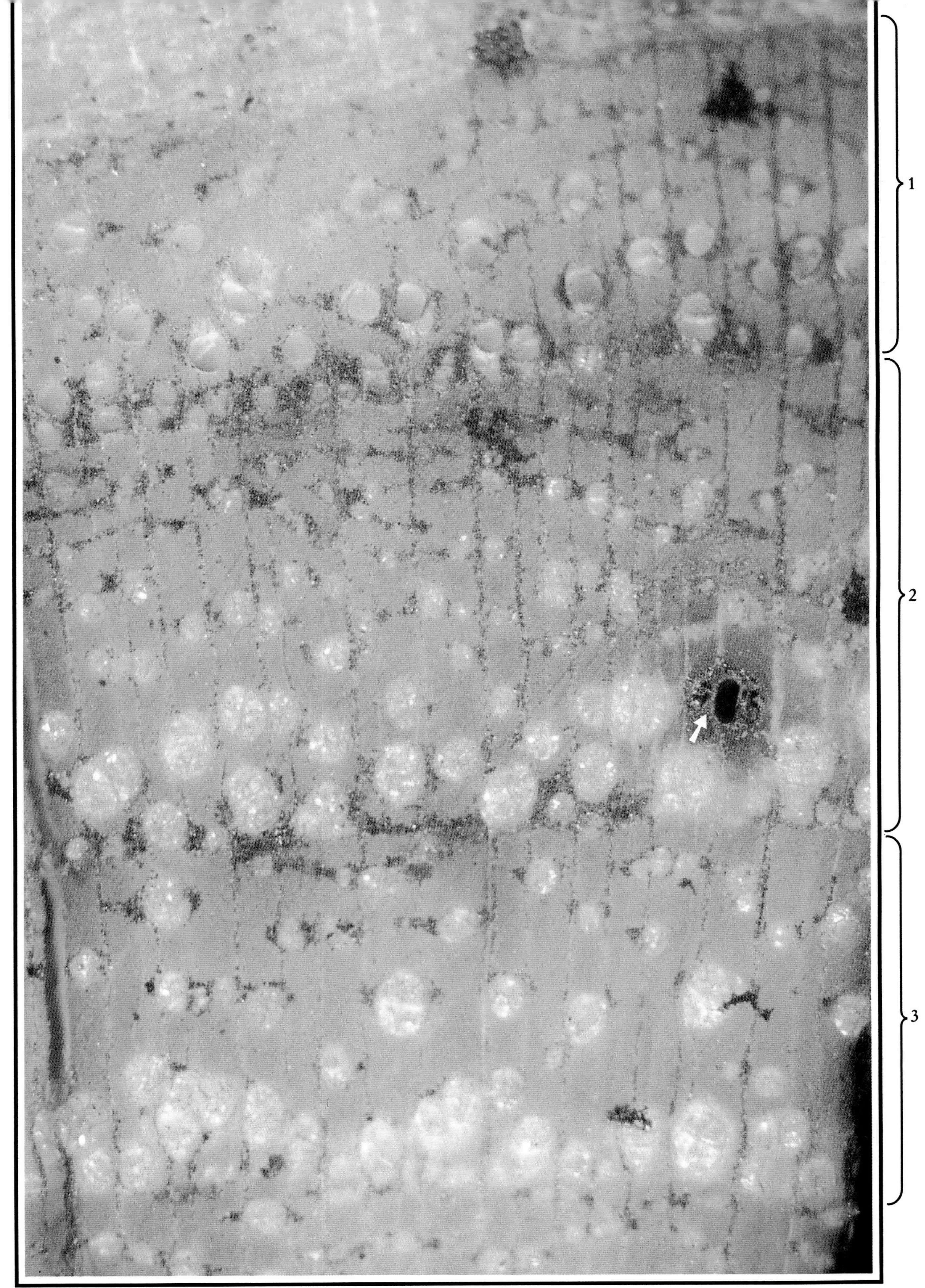

Black Locust, *Robinia pseudoacacia*

Only the current growth increment has open vessels (1). It is conducting sapwood. Increments 2 and 3 have vessels plugged by masses of small tyloses. They are non-conducting sapwood. The arrow shows a vessel without tyloses. An infection killed the axial parenchyma that would have formed the tyloses. Toluidine blue and iodine were flooded on the sample to enhance the sparkle of the tyloses and to show the symplast as a dark blue network.

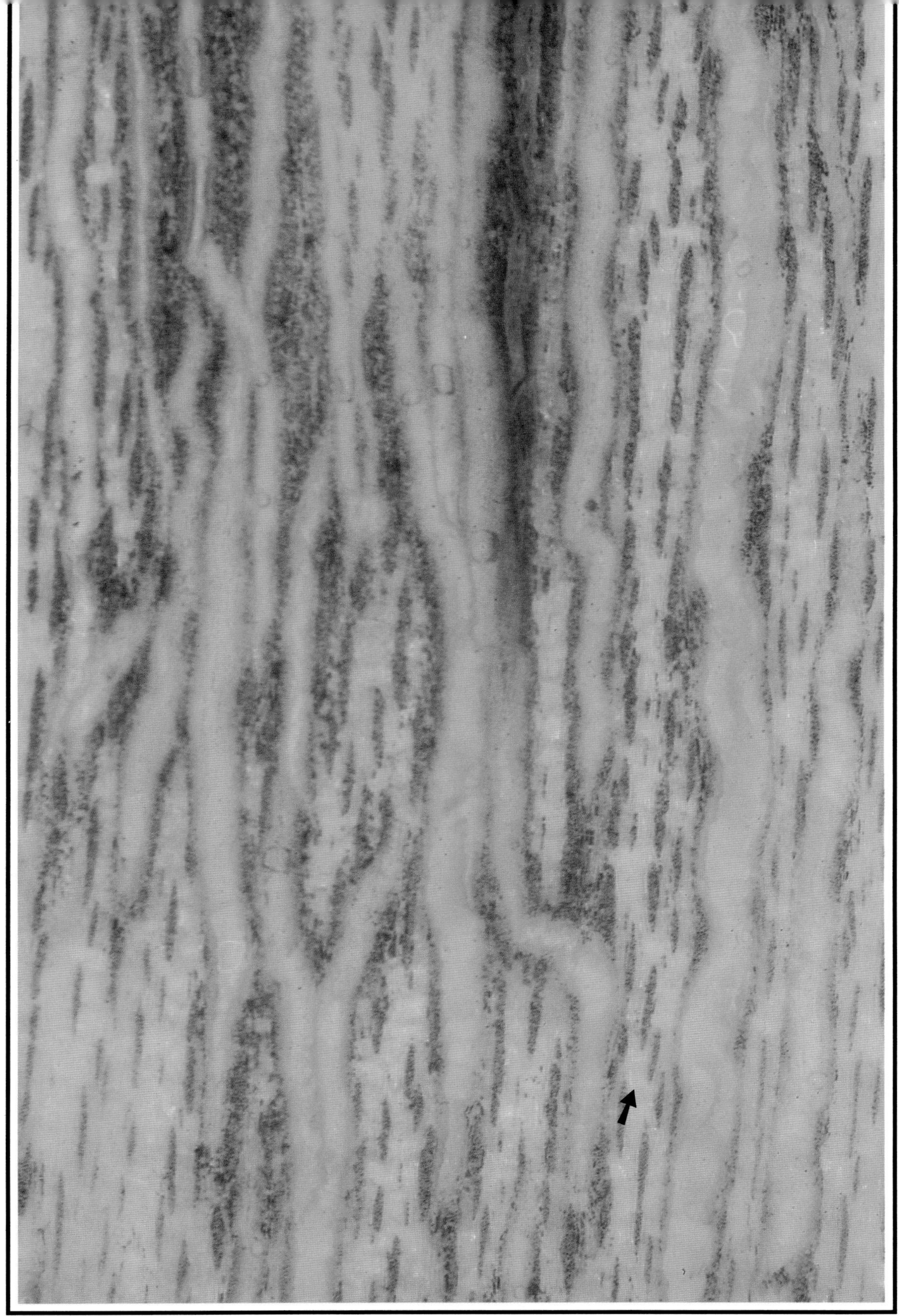

Black Locust, *Robinia pseudoacacia*

An iodine-stained tangential dissection shows the curving and connecting open vessels in the current growth increment. The arrow points to a spindle-shaped ray as seen cut at a right angle to the radial parenchyma cells. Note the abundance of axial parenchyma that surrounds the vessels.

Vessels do end. Vessels weave through the wood and often connect at their ends with other vessels.

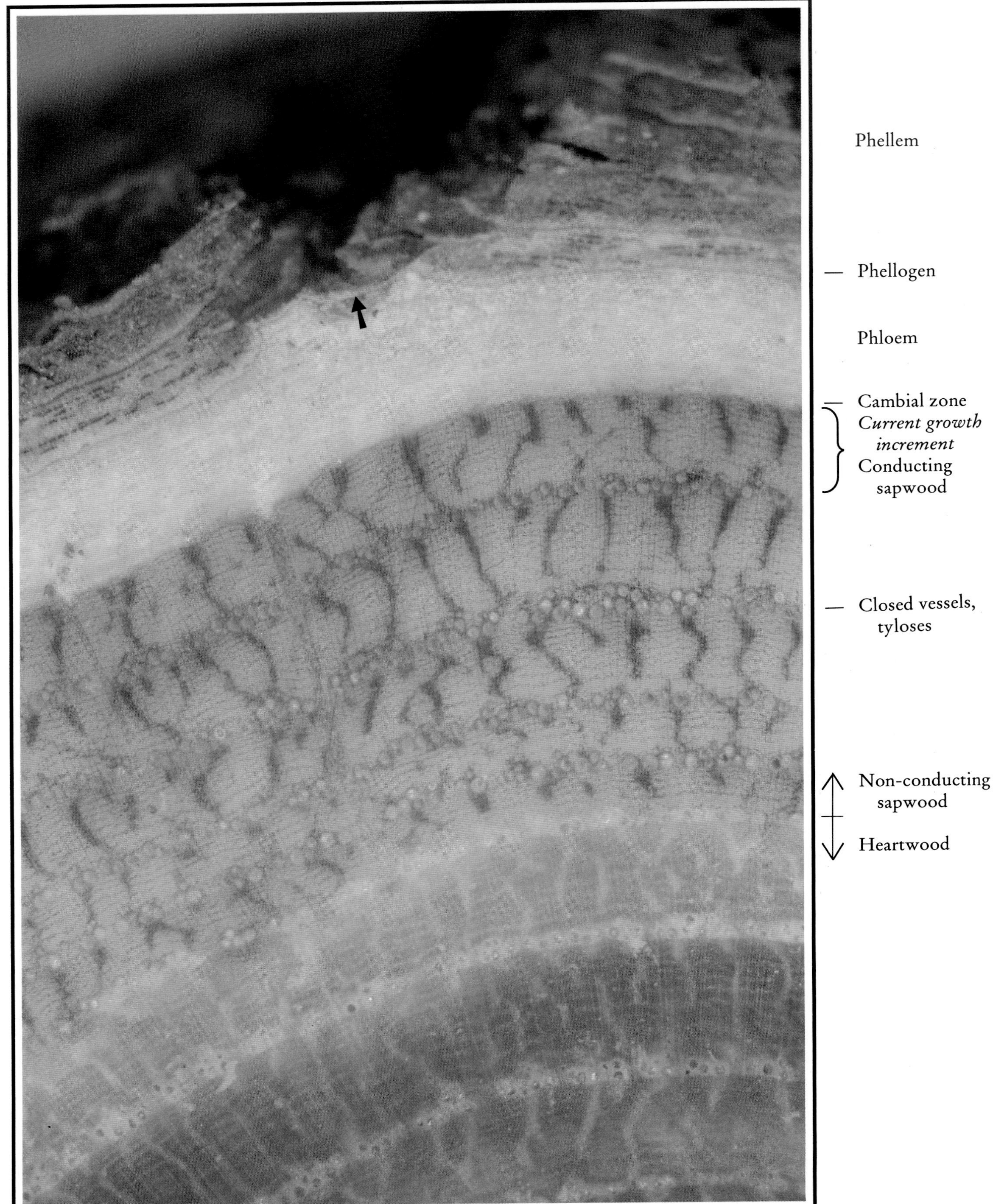

Bur Oak, *Quercus macrocarpa*

Compare this sample from an old bur oak with the sample from a young bur oak on page 43. When heartwood-forming trees are young they usually have many growth increments of sapwood. As the trees mature the number of sapwood increments decrease and remain stable. The sample above has one growth increment of conducting sapwood and 4 increments of non-conducting sapwood. The arrow shows a patch of green tissue in a fissure. The outer bark is made up of layers of corky phellem. The plates of phellem form as new phellogens form deeper within the phloem and push the older phellogen with its phellem outward. The thick plates of phellem are called the rhytidome.

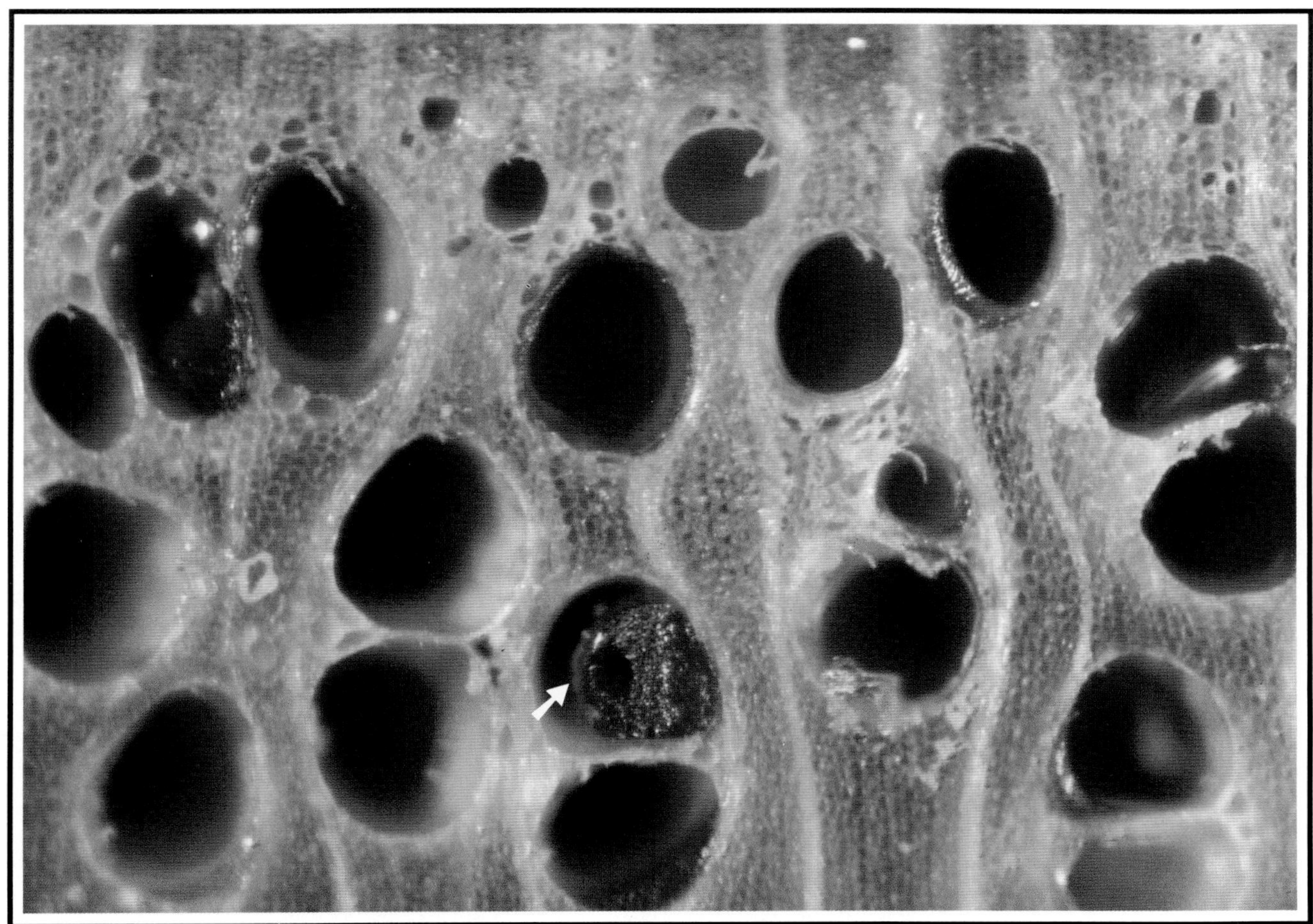

Chinaberry Tree, ***Melia azedarach***

The arrow points to a ruby red inclusion in the vessel. Vessels of chinaberry may also contain tyloses. The tree produces medicinal substances that are narcotic, and deadly to insects, especially fleas and mosquitoes. Many trees produce medicinal substances that do benefit humankind in many ways. The nature of potentially beneficial properties of many of the inclusions in wood and bark are poorly understood. The saddest part of this story is that some of the trees that are called weeds may have some of the most valuable substances. And they are the first to be cut.

One growth increment
Earlywood Latewood

Douglas Fir, *Pseudotsuga menziesii*
The earlywood took the toluidine blue stain very heavily while the latewood hardly stained. This is so because the earlywood tracheids have thin walls, and large openings that took the stain. The latewood tracheids have very thick walls and small openings that took less of the stain. The non-staining thick walls of the latewood tracheids contrast with the thin walls of the earlywood tracheids.

Conifers have transport cells that are called tracheids. Conifers do not have vessels. Tracheids are spindle-shaped cells that have small pore-like openings on their sides. The openings are called pits. The pits between tracheids make transport of liquids possible.

→

Growth rate decreasing

Douglas Fir, *Pseudotsuga menziesii*

The sample was flooded with iodine stain and then photographed. Note the decrease in the widths of the growth increments. The rays are very numerous, but because they are so thin they are difficult to see. Very little starch was in the ray parenchyma.

The decrease in growth rate indicates a problem that started 9 or 10 years before the tree was cut. When trees die, an "autopsy" can give valuable information that could benefit trees that are still alive. Too often by the time symptoms of decline are noted, it is too late for effective treatment.

Black Mangrove, *Avicennia germinans*

The blue stain developed naturally 3 weeks after the sample was cut. The pattern of growth increments is very different from any seen in temperate-climate species. The several genera of mangroves grow in and along salt coastal ways and inlets, and they also grow in fresh water, and on land. A very versatile group of plants! The stem of the tree contains xylem and strips of phloem-like tissues. They join and "run" without any definite pattern. In a strange sense, many tropical trees are like overlapping annuals with xylem and phloem repeating within the stem or trunk. Mangroves; black, *Avicennia* species; red. *Rhizophora* species; and white *Laguncularia racemosa*, a monotypic genus, all have many similar characteristics. They do grow in brackish water that contains as much salt as sea water, but no more. The xylem sap contains high amounts of salt that moves to the surface of the leaves.

Right. **Bougainvillea,** *Bougainvillea* sp.

A vine, a shrub, a small tree. Bougainvillea is another woody plant that has bands of phloem or soft bark (pink-blue) within the xylem (green-blue). Again, the anatomy of many topical trees and other woody plants is different from temperate-climate trees. The sample was stained with toluidine blue. The woody members of the four-o'clock family (Nyctaginaceae) have "included phloem" in the wood. Wood species of *Guapira* and *Pisonia* also have this feature.

TROPICAL WOODS

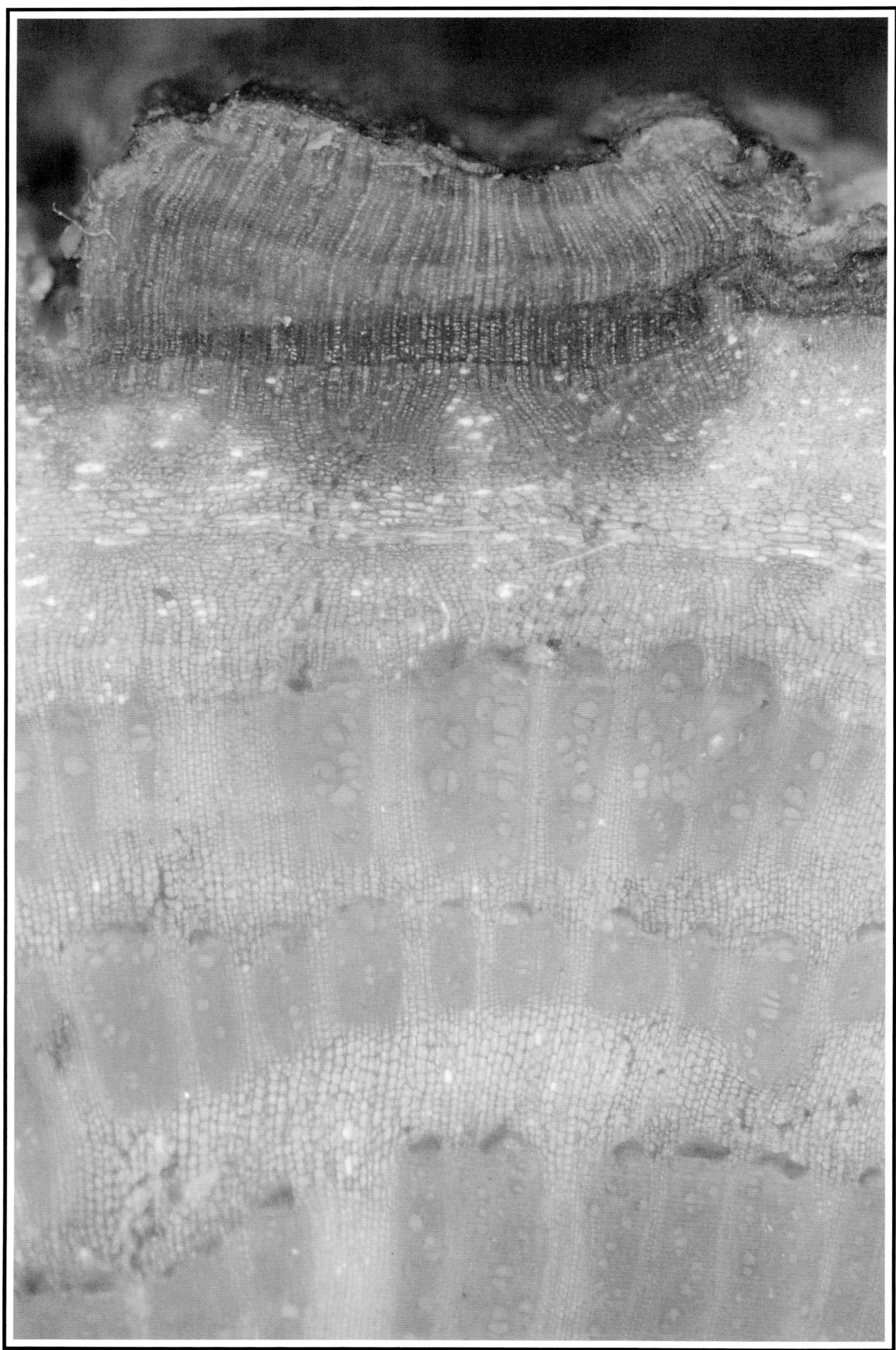

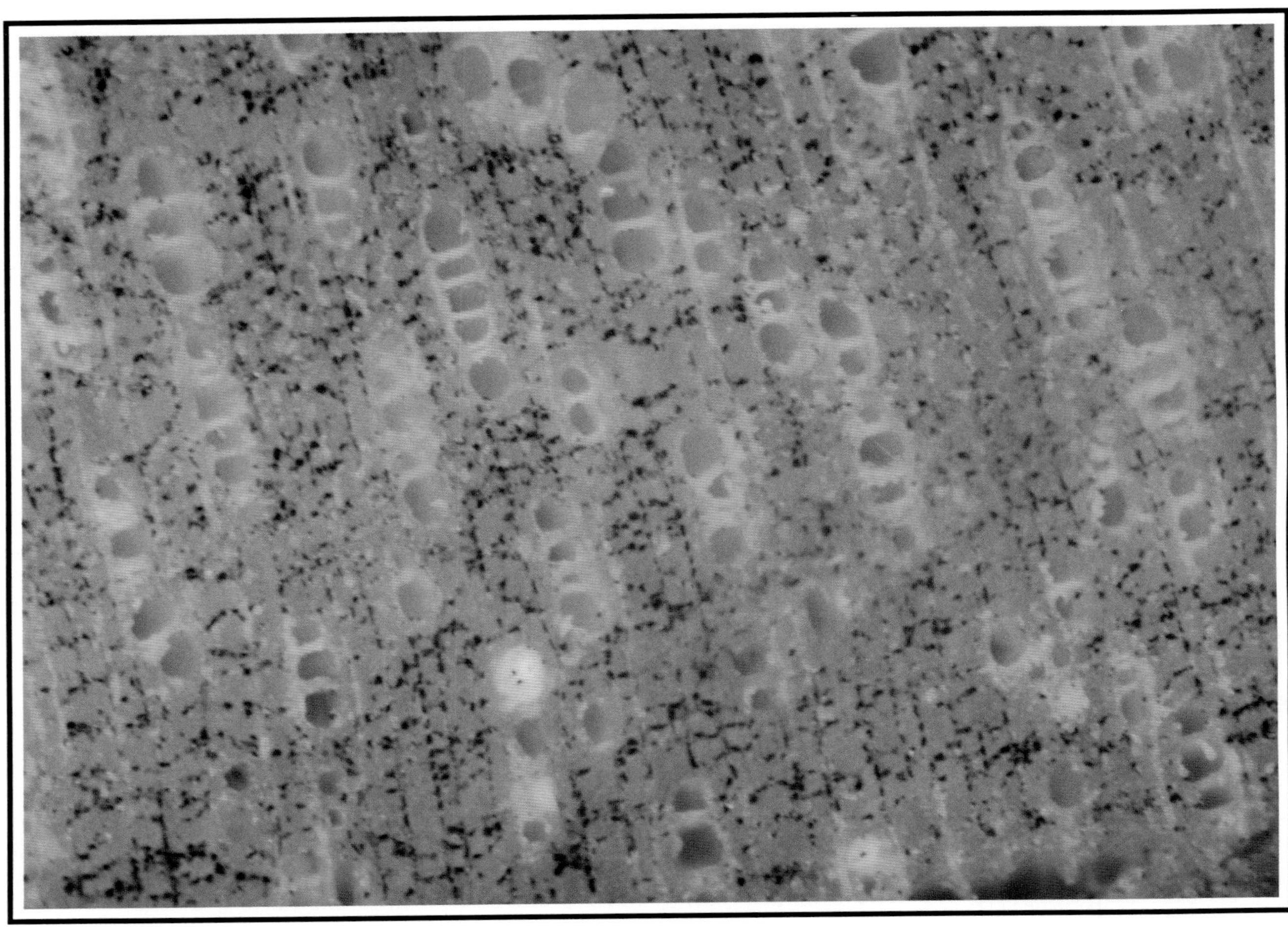

False Mastic, *Masticodendron foetidissimum*

Many tropical trees store an abundance of starch in wood, as shown in this sample stained with iodine. The pattern of small-diameter vessels joined with others in radial rows is common in many tropical species. This tree, and many other tropical species do not have distinctive growth increments.

Right. **Coral Tree,** *Erythrina flabelliformis*

The coral tree is a very fast growing tree with moderately soft wood. The tree produces an abundance of large showy flowers. Vessels, as singles and joined multiples, are scattered throughout the wood. Bands of phloem-like cells (blue) are interspersed with more dense xylem (green-blue). The sample was stained with toluidine blue. Iodine staining of other samples showed very heavy starch reserves. Tropical trees, unlike their cold-climate cousins, must maintain a year-round defense system. This means that a great amount of energy must be stored for defense. And, because many tropical trees have an abundance of large flowers and fruit, more energy is required for reproduction. Some tropical trees have very dense woods so packed with extractives and other substances that the wood does not float. The point is that tropical trees have very high energy demands throughout the year.

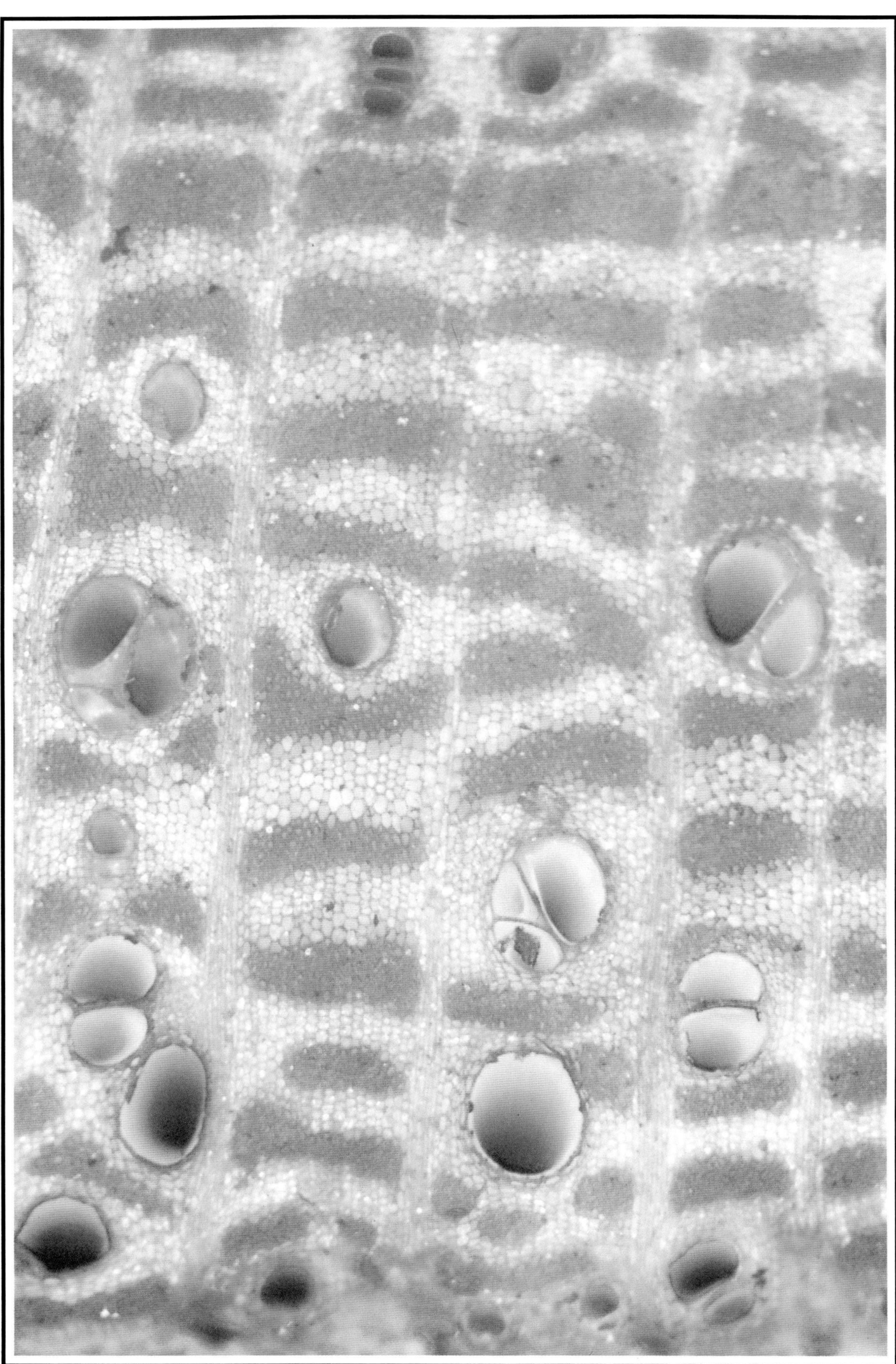

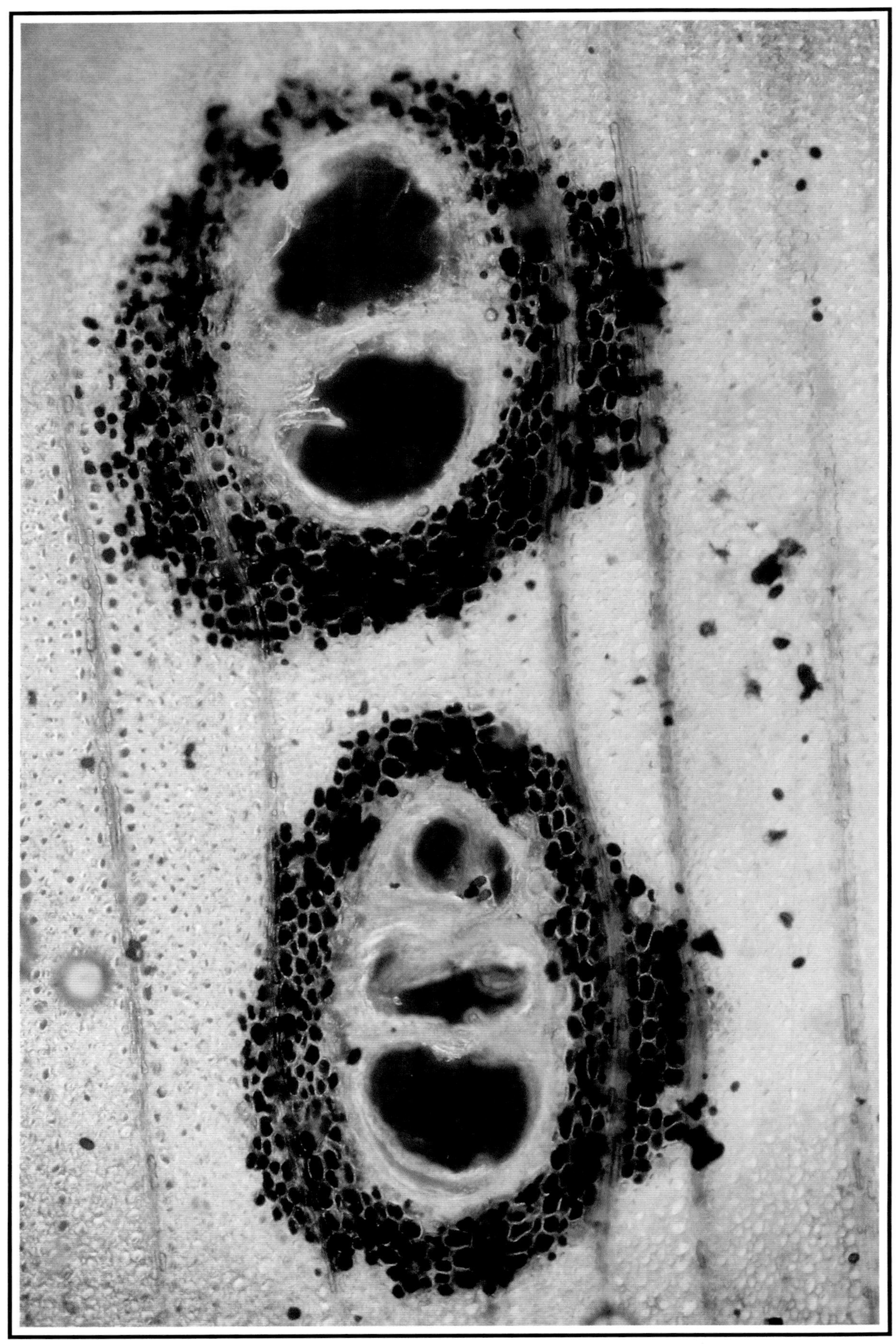

Mango, *Mangifera indica*

Mango is a very tough tree in the sense of survival after injuries. It is usually severely mutilated in orchards to facilitate the harvesting of fruit. Its toughness may be because of its ability to store high amounts of starch. This iodine stained, back-lighted photograph shows the abundance of starch-filled cells surrounding the vessels.

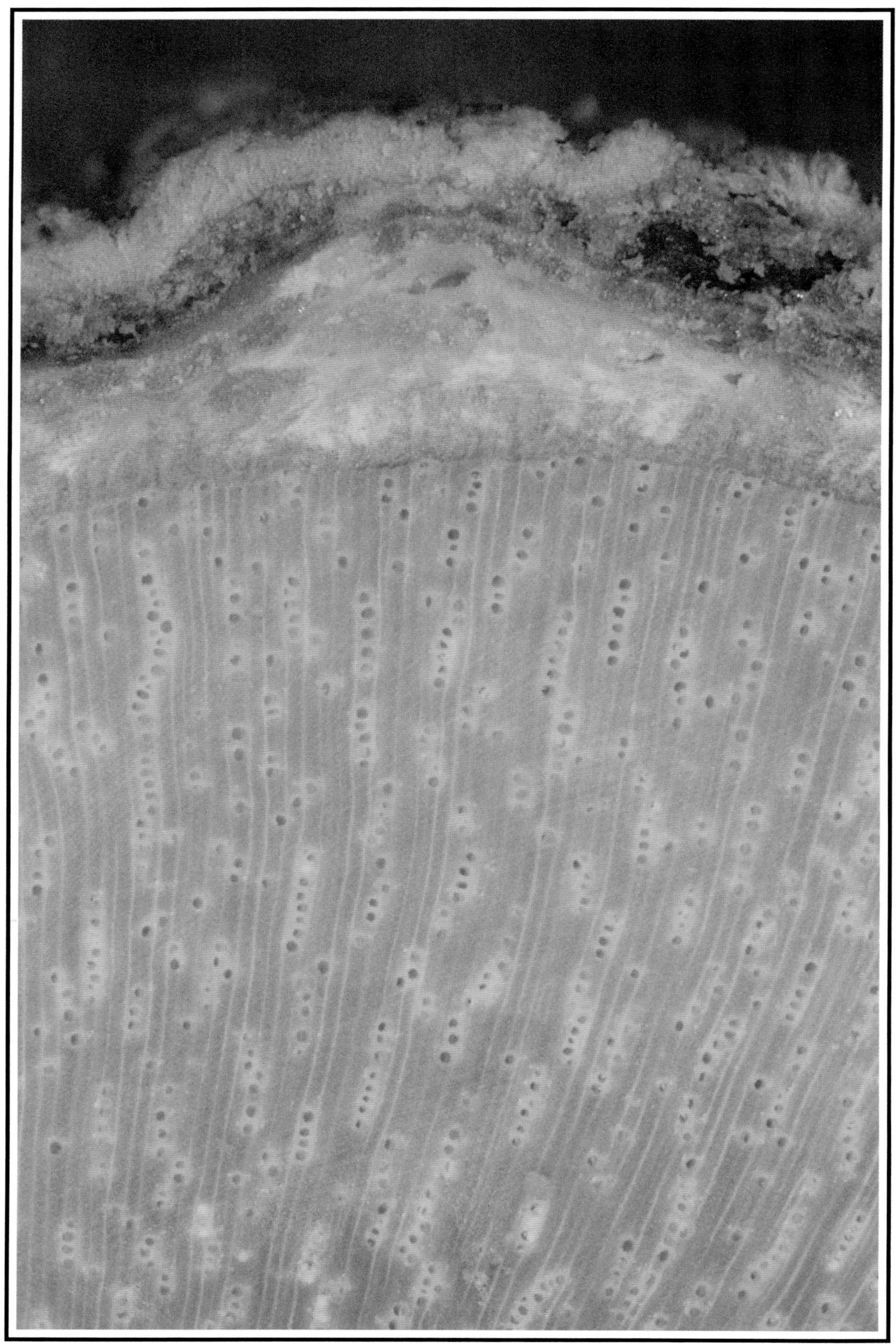

Bulnesia, *Bulnesia arborea*

Dense, hard wood, small vessels joined in radial rows, and inner bark with an abundance of chlorophyll are characteristics of many tropical trees. The specific gravity of these dense woods is often near one or even over one in some cases.

This tree belongs to the Lignum-vitae family, Zygophyllaceae. The creosote bush, *Larrea divaricata,* also belongs to this family. A creosote bush found in California is thought to be the oldest living plant in the world.

TRUNK AND ROOT WOOD COMPARISON

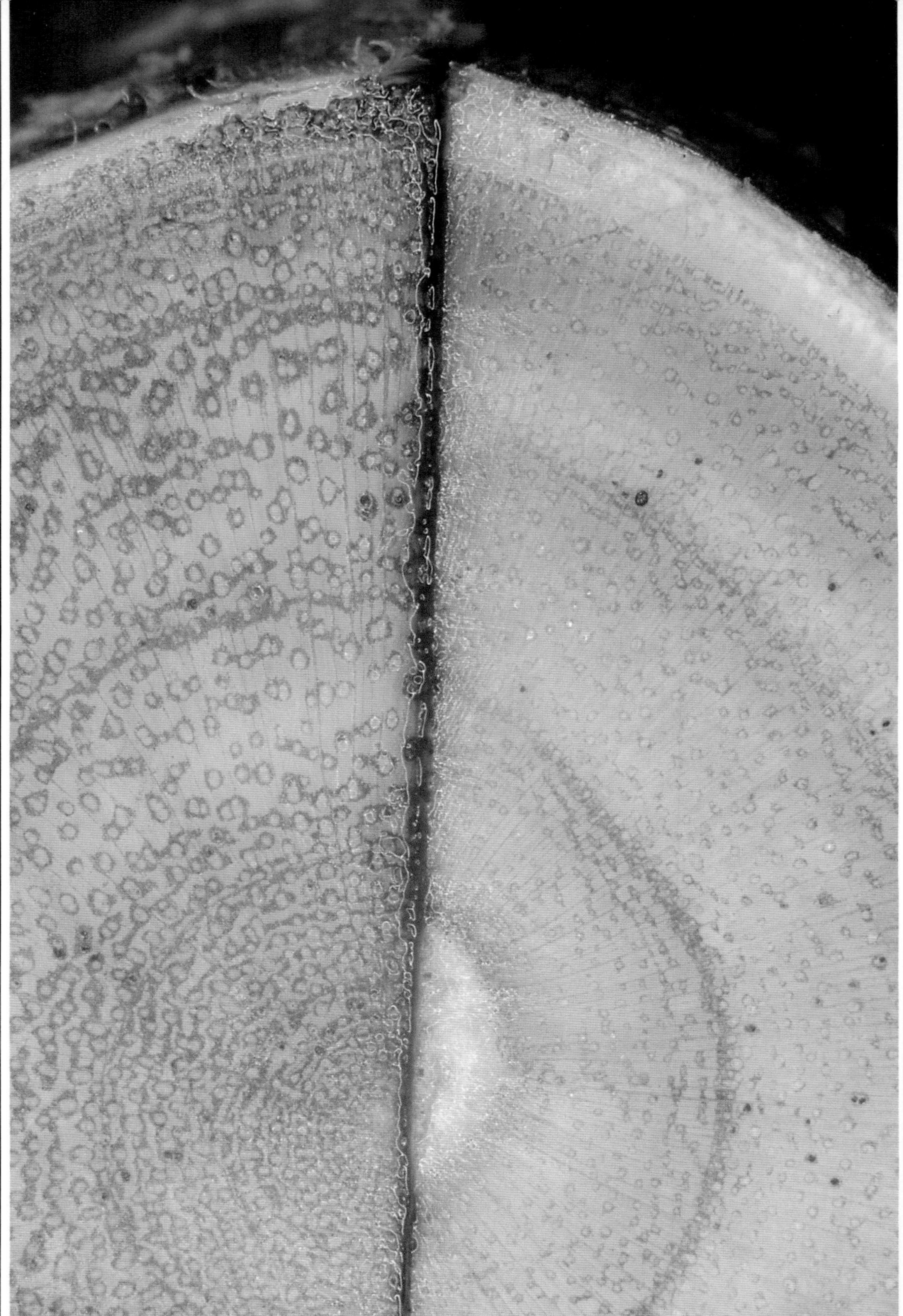

ROOT STEM

Honey Locust, *Gleditsia triacanthos*
The root has no chlorophyll in its bark, but the inner bark stores starch. The stem has an abundance of cells with chlorophyll. The root has large vessels with abundance of starch in parenchyma surrounding the vessels. Stem has smaller vessels with much less starch in parenchyma surrounding the vessels. Root has no pith. Stem has a pith. Root has moderate amount of lignin in cell walls. Stem has high amount of lignin in cell walls.

Right. **Honey Locust**, *Gleditsia triacanthos*
A closer view of the root shows large vessels surrounded by parenchyma cells that are full of starch. The axial parenchyma surrounding the vessels connects with the radial parenchyma of the rays. Roots require a great amount of stored energy to power their growth. Roots cannot trap energy.

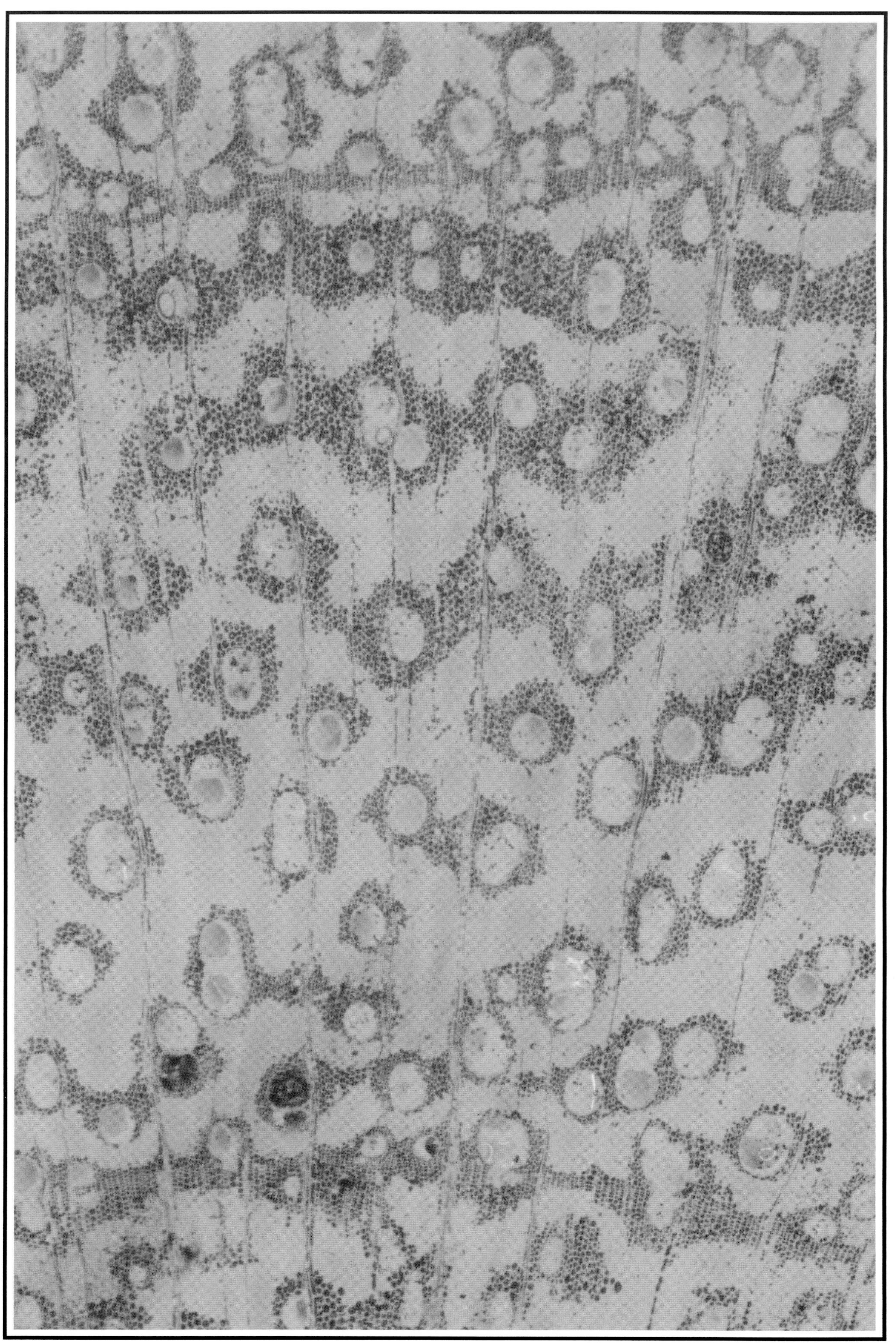

CALLUS

Neem Tree, ***Azadirachta indica***

Callus is forming between the cut woody root at left and the shredded bark at right on this longitudinally dissected sample from a neem tree. Callus is a growth of homogeneous cells that have little lignin in their walls, and the cells are meristematic, which means they have the ability to divide and to differentiate into a distinct organ — root, shoot, flower.

Callus can form when wounds expose still living cells in the cambial zone or rays of radial parenchyma in wood. It is common to see callus on the surface of shallow wounds where only the bark was removed. The neem tree is widely planted in India. The tree produces substances that are insecticidal.

MERISTEMATIC POINTS

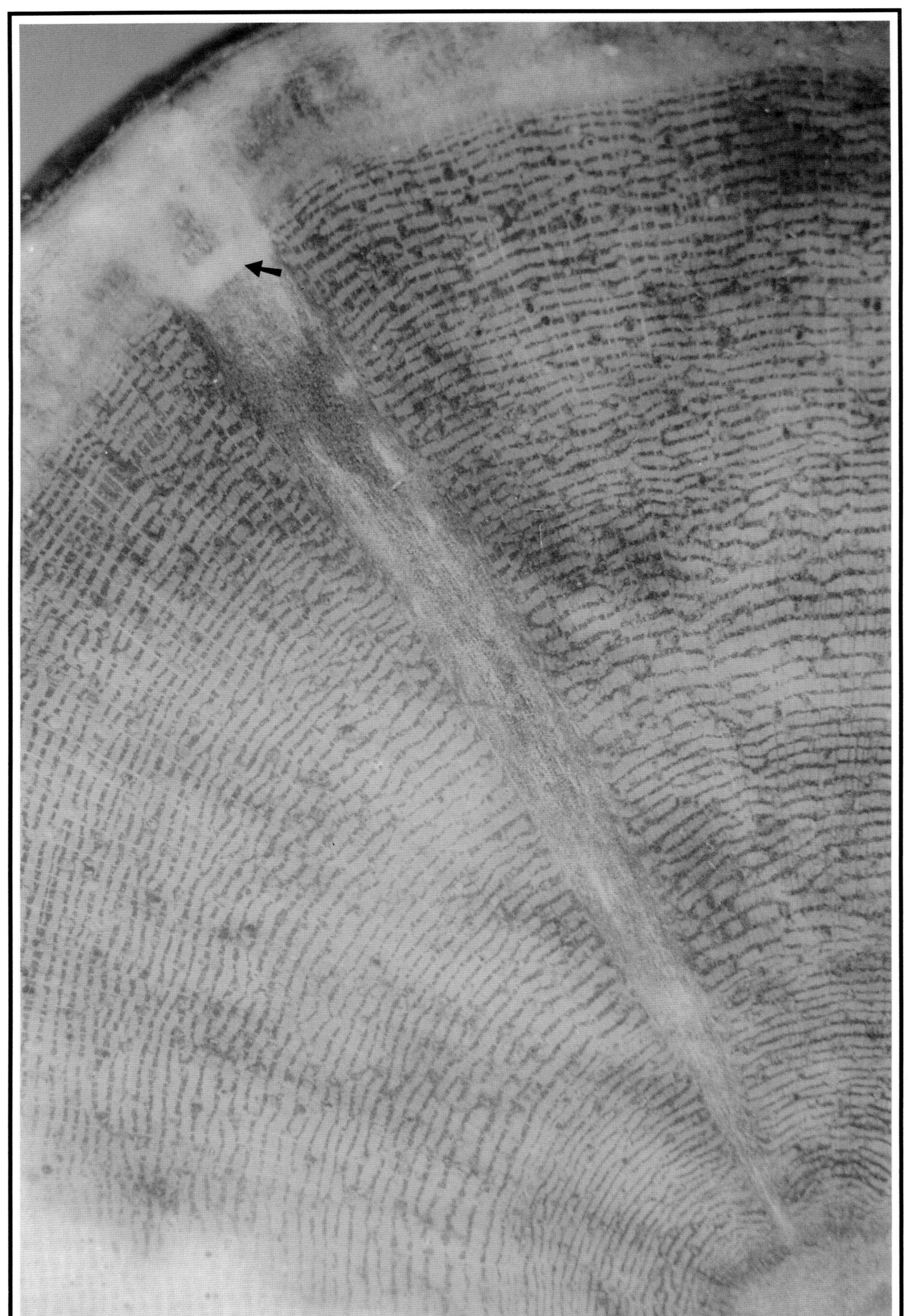

Weeping Fig, ***Ficus benjamina***

Clusters of radial parenchyma make up an expanding tube-like structure that terminates in the cambial zone with a thick layer of meristematic cells that do not store starch (arrow). Meristems do not store starch. The tube-like structures appear as giant rays. I call them meristematic points. They are common in most tree trunks and roots. They have been called bud traces. A bud is a structure made up of differentiated tissues. Meristematic points do not have differentiated tissues, but they do have the capacity to form them. Meristematic points can form roots, prop roots, sprouts, or flowers. Iodine staining shows the abundant starch in the meristematic point, and also the abundance of starch in the living cells in the wood — symplast.

Black Walnut, *Juglans nigra*

A meristematic point in black walnut. The bark was pulled away from the wood. The bark was cut, but the wood was not. The point protrudes into the bark and is enclosed in a "crown" of phellem. Green tissues are within the "crown". But there is no bud there. Meristematic points are very common in black walnut. The points can protrude a centimeter into the bark. My point is that they do not terminate in a bud. A bud is a preformed structure. However, a meristematic point can differentiate to form a sprout, flower or root. And if the sprout or flower grows and dies, more meristematic points may then form or true buds may develop to form a burl or swollen structure on the trunk. Structures that form from callus or meristematic points are called adventitious. Structures that form from differentiated tissues that did not grow the season they were formed are called dormant buds. Any structure that forms on a tree after primary growth is called epicormic. Adventitious and dormant define the type of epicormic structure.

Right. **American Beech,** *Fagus grandifolia*

When woody roots are pruned, where do the new woody roots come from? Some come from callus that forms about the cut and others come from meristematic points.

Woody roots do not come from buds, so roots cannot have dormant buds or latent buds, or buds of any kind for woody roots. The dissected beech root was stained with iodine. The central portion of the root that did not take the stain was the diameter of the root when it was wounded. Many of the vessels in this zone were plugged with a fibrillar substance. The plugs are not tyloses. After the wound, one meristematic point began to differentiate to form a new woody root.

Callus associated with root injuries or meristematic points may differentiate to form root shoots on many species of woody plants.

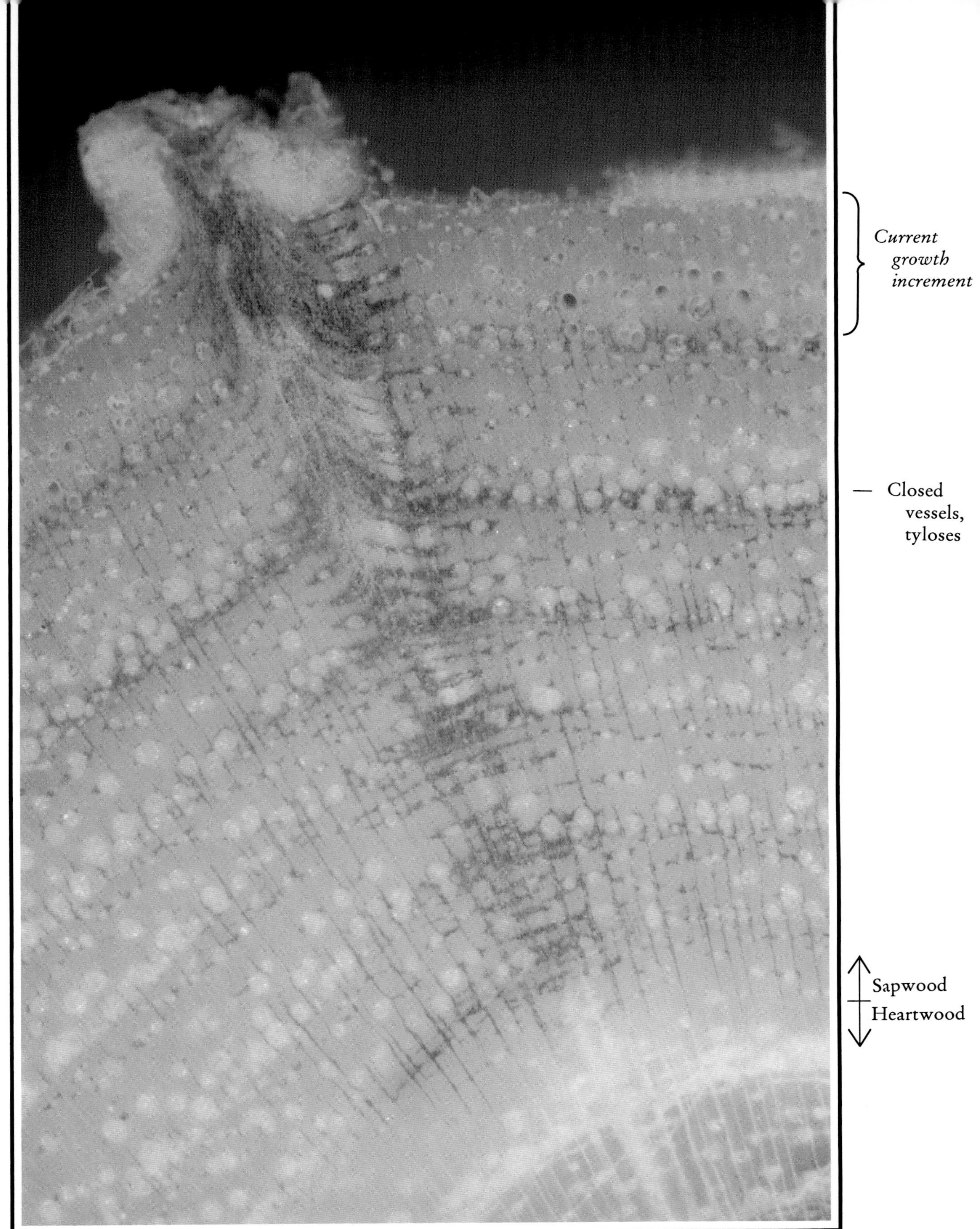

Black Locust, *Robinia pseudoacacia*
Meristematic points have an abundance of starch as shown in this iodine-stained sample of a black locust stem The abundance of starch helps to explain why vigorous-appearing sprouts often form on declining trees. The sprouts have a "built in" ready energy source. A sprout formed and died leaving a raised structure that contains tissues similar to callus. New sprouts could form from this raised structure. I believe that a decrease in energy reserves in tissues near meristematic points is the trigger that initiates action to begin forming a sprout. On many tropical trees flowers and fruit form on trunks of mature trees. Again, they start from meristematic points similar to those shown here.

ROOTS

There are two basic types of roots: Woody and non-woody.

Woody roots are organs that mechanically support the tree, store energy reserves, and transport liquids that contain many types of soluble substances. Woody roots have lignin along with cellulose and hemicelluloses in their cell walls. Woody roots have an outer bark that contains suberin. Suberin gives bark its corky characteristic. Suberin "waterproofs" the tissues. Woody roots have secondary growth. Woody roots contain meristematic points. Woody roots usually grow outward and downward. New woody root tissues begin to grow soon after woody growth starts in the trunk.

Non-woody roots are organs that absorb water and elements essential for growth. Further, there are two types of structures that form on or in non-woody roots: root hairs and mycorrhizae. Root hairs are organs that are extensions of epidermal cells. Mycorrhizae are organs composed of tree and fungus tissue, a composite structure. Non-woody roots have very little lignin in cell walls. Non-woody roots live for a short time; from a few weeks to a year. Some mycorrhizae "regrow" on themselves and may grow for more than a year. Root hairs come fast, and go fast. As conditions occur that support their growth, they grow. Root hairs are most common on young plants and plants growing in containers. Root hairs are not so common on most mature trees, and especially forest trees.

There are two basic types of mycorrhizae: those in which fungal cells infect the outermost cells of the mycorrhizae and those in which fungal cells infect all the cells of the mycorrhizae internally. Those that have infections primarily in the outermost cells are called ectomycorrhizae. Those that have all cells infected internally are called endomycorrhizae. As is the case most of the time in natural systems, gradations from one extreme to another usually exist. Those structures that have some characteristics between the two types given are called ectendomycorrhizae.

Some endomycorrhiaze form vesicles and other types of structures in the non-woody root cells. These mycorrhizae are called vesicular-arbuscular mycorrhizae or VA mycorrhizae. The roots infected by the VA fungi appear similar to normal, non-infected non-woody roots. To see the fungi, sections must be stained and examined under the microscope.

The uniqueness of the mychorrhizae lies in their ability to readily absorb elements such as phosphorus, zinc, manganese, and copper. How much is absorbed through the tree tissue part of the mycorrhiza and through the hyphae of the fungus portion of the mycorrhiza is not well understood. The mycorrhiza is the organ, the structure. However, the fungi associated with the structure often form hyphae — vegetative tubes of a fungus — far beyond the structure. And, again, how much of the absorption is directly into the structure and how much enters through the hyphae growing away from the structure is not well understood.

Now, let us look at some of the structures discussed here.

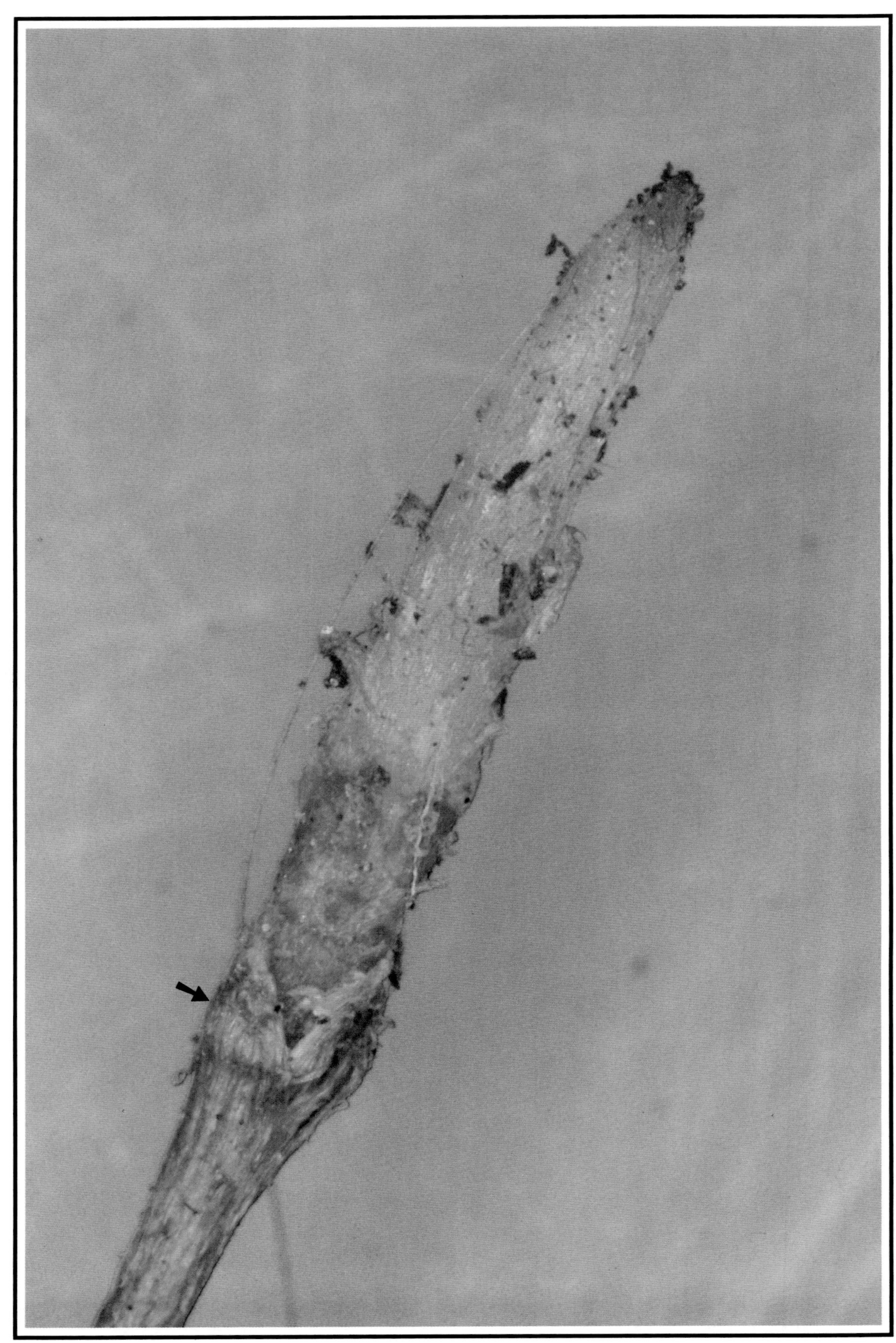

Canadian Hemlock, *Tsuga canadensis*
A newly formed "pioneer" root emerges from a calyx-like structure (arrow) at the end of a hemlock root. These large spear-like roots grow for long distances before branching roots form. These roots seldom have root hairs. Root hairs and mycorrhizae usually form on the branching roots. The new pioneer root is usually twice the diameter of the root that generated it. The red tip is natural, the root was not stained. These spear-like roots are common on conifers.

Canadian Hemlock, *Tsuga canadensis*

The root hairs are beginning to die and turn brown. At the same time the non-woody root is starting to become a woody root. A root hair is the extension of a single epidermal cell. The root hair is not the entire root section. Non-woody roots that have thousands of root hairs are often incorrectly called a root hair.

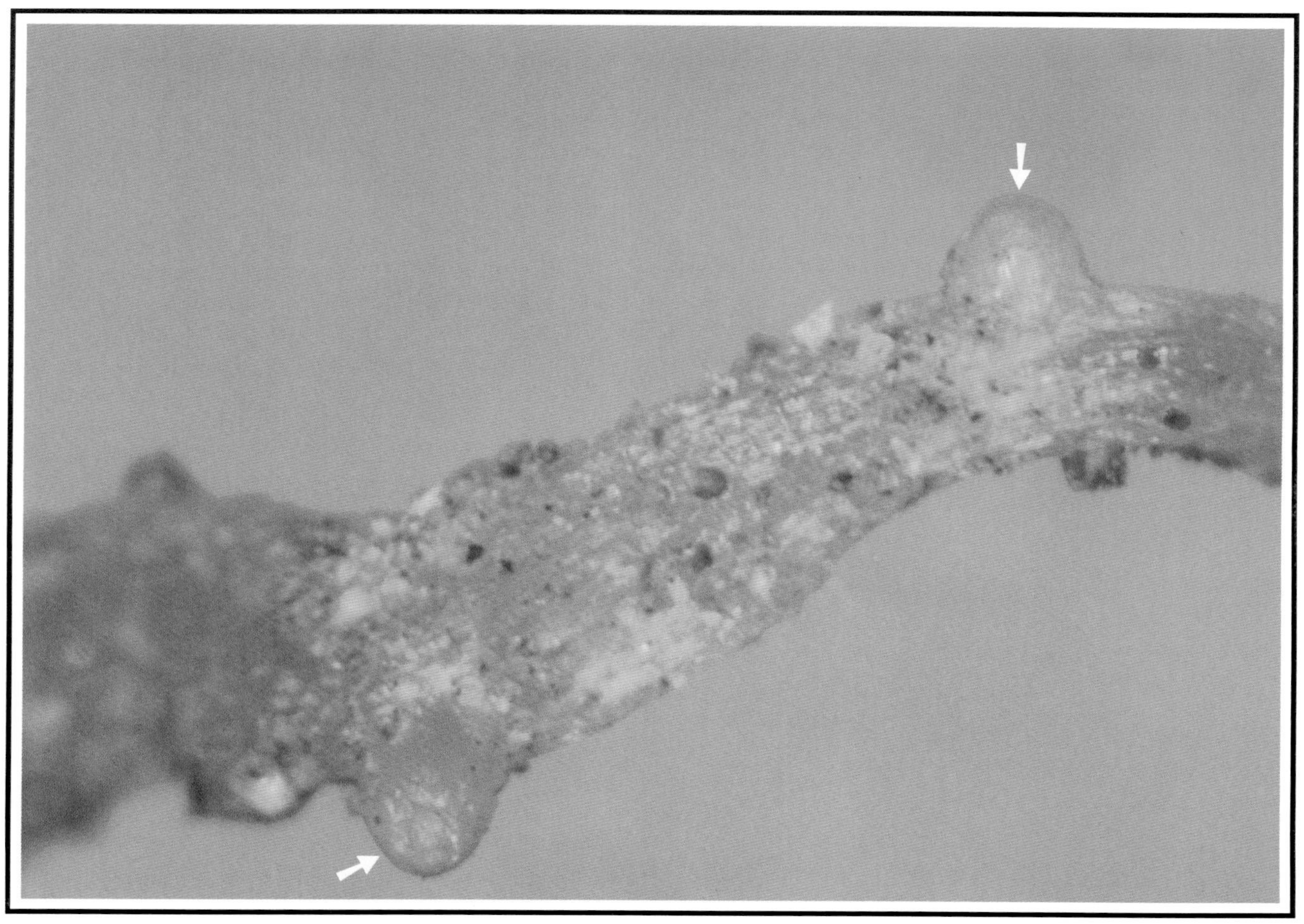

Canadian Hemlock, *Tsuga canadensis*

The arrows show the beginning of new non-woody roots. If the new roots are not infected by fungi, they will go on to form roots with root hairs. If the young forming roots are infected, then they will begin to form mycorrhizae. Sometimes the infection takes place after a root hair zone has started. Then some root hairs may be seen on the mycorrhiza or on the non-woody root that hold it. (Canadian hemlock was used for these studies because it was easy to lift them off of a rock and to be certain that the structures studied were part of the root system. The tree could then easily be laid back on its rock. Hemlocks commonly grow on granite boulders.)

Left. **Canadian Hemlock**, *Tsuga canadensis*

As a non-woody root grows and starts to become woody, the epidermal cells and root hairs are shed. The shedding cells are readily infected by waiting fungi (arrow). The shedding of dead root hairs, epidermal cells, and mycorrhizae ensure a continuing supply of organic material — mulch? —for trees, especially trees planted in cities where asphalt or concrete cover the roots. The fungi that digest the dead materials are not the ones that form the mycorrhizae.

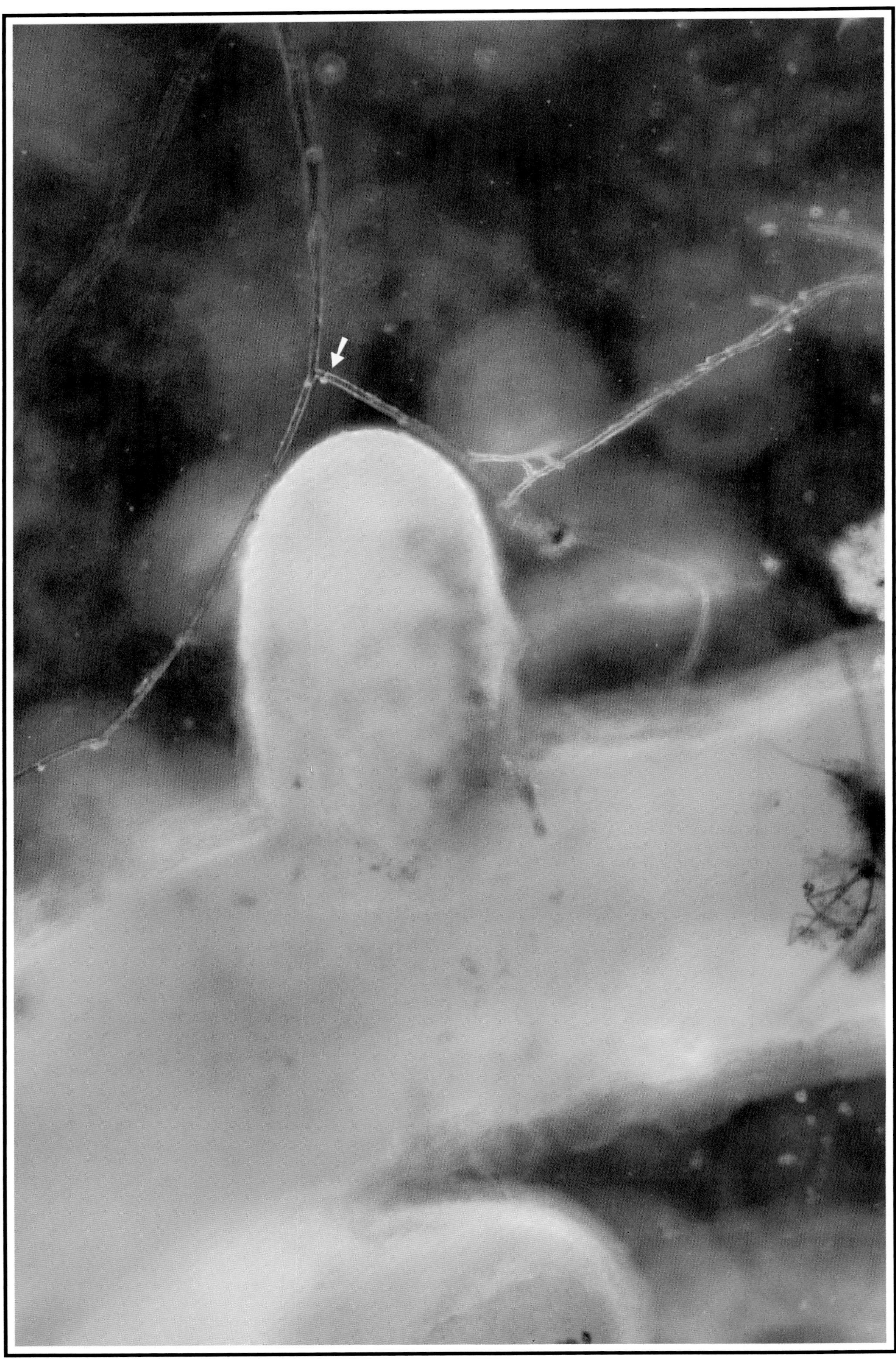

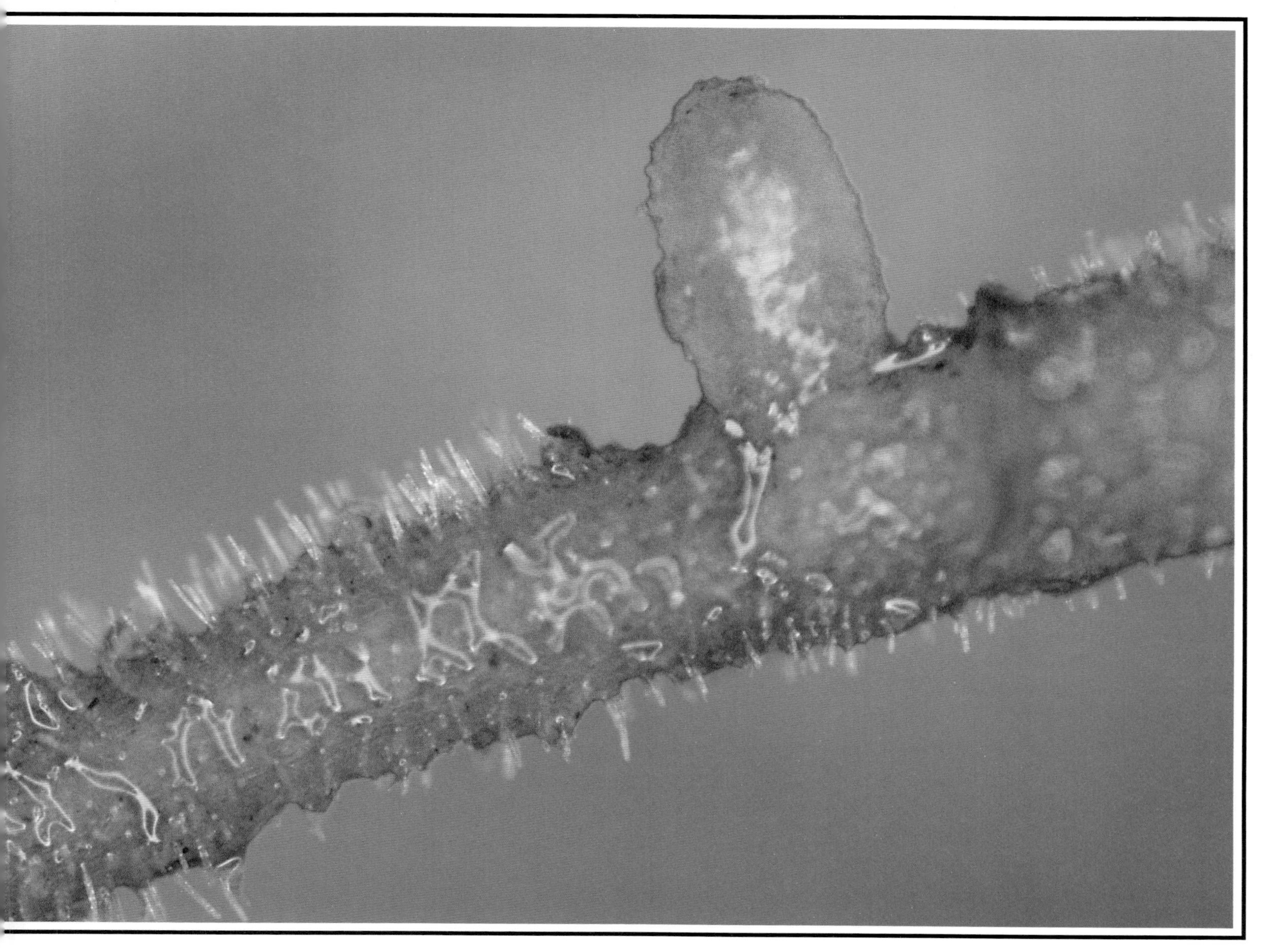

Canadian Hemlock, *Tsuga canadensis*
New root hairs and a young developing mycorrhizae on a hemlock non-woody root. This sample was collected in winter 1993 in New Hampshire. The sample was in non-frozen soil only a centimeter below frozen soil. Many samples taken in winter showed the same features.

Left. **Canadian Hemlock,** *Tsuga canadensis*
A back-lighted photograph showing the hyphae of a fungus growing near an emerging non-woody root. The arrow points to a structure called a clamp connection, which indicates that the fungus was a member of the Basidiomycota. Hyphae of many types of fungi are extremely abundant in soil, especially in the upper organic layers.

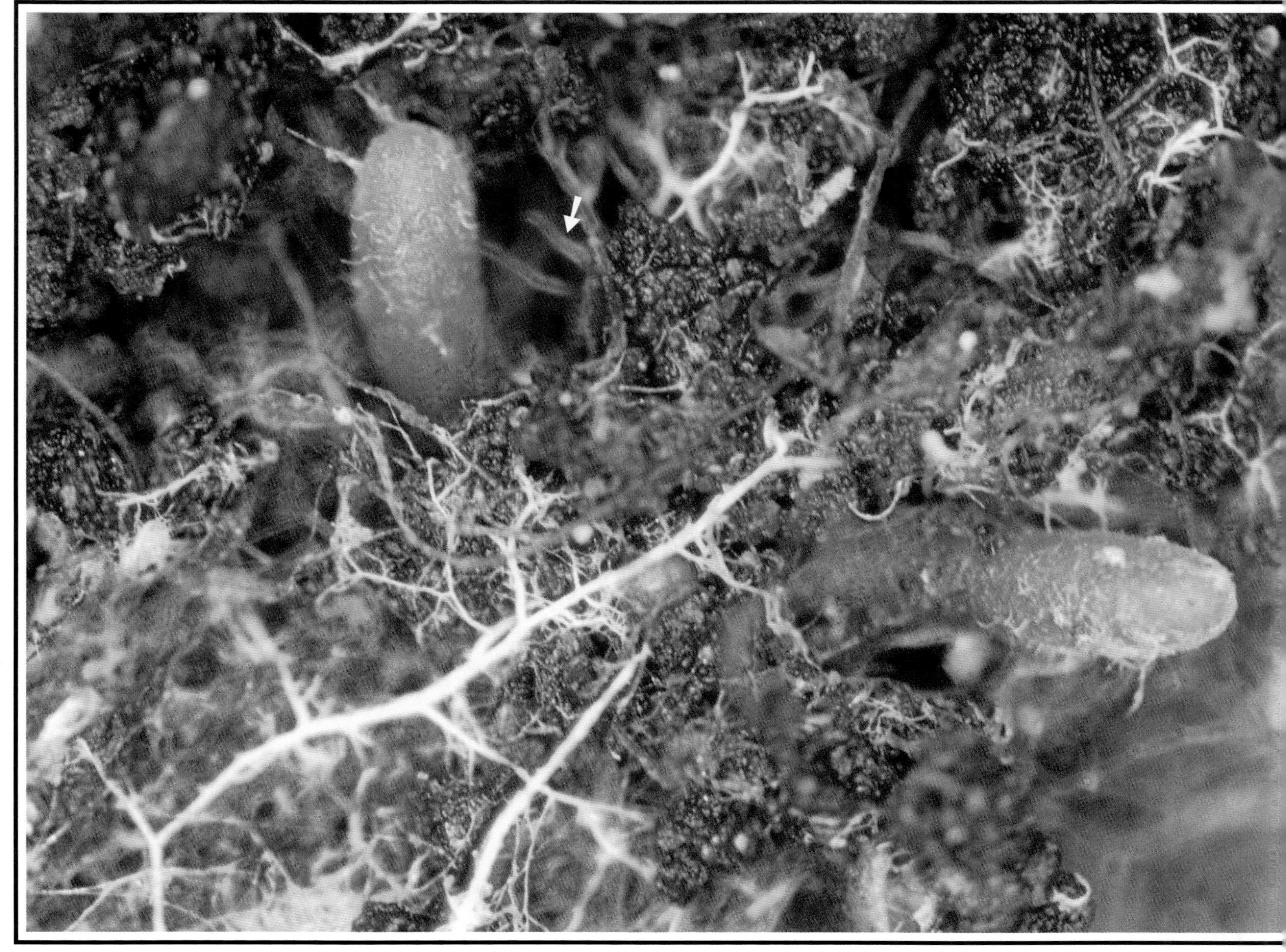

Canadian Hemlock, *Tsuga canadensis*

A frozen layer of soil was peeled back from the non-frozen soil shown here. The mycorrhizae were growing into the space that separated frozen soil from non-frozen. The white "ropes" are strands of hyphae of fungi that digest dead leaves and twigs. The arrow shows a small worm. Thrips are common in the soils in winter. On pine roots, scale insects are often found and their waxy coverings or strands can be mistaken for hyphae of fungi. I have seen scale insects on white pine roots, *Pinus strobus*, and Douglas fir roots, *Pseudotsuga menziesii.*

Right. **Mycorrhizae In A Small Cavity**

Mycorrhizae commonly grow upright into small cavities in the soil. When soils are compacted the cavities are destroyed. And when the cavities are destroyed, so are the mycorrhizae. Yes, lack of air and water are problems in compacted soil. However, even more important is that the micro habitats for mycorrhizae are destroyed. Adding composted leaf and twig mulch would help to restore habitats for mycorrhizae. When mycorrhizae are destroyed, the tree could develop deficiencies for essential elements, especially phosphorus.

Eastern White Pine, ***Pinus strobus***

Soil particles often adhere to the non-woody roots as shown here. The root hairs are brown and no longer functional. Patches of white mycelium — fungus hyphae — are on the non-woody root. The mycorrhizae have forked, clear tips, typical of those that are on conifers. Note that mycorrhizae and root hairs are growing from the same non-woody root. When looking for mycorrhizae, look for clods of soil that look like grapes on a cluster. Carefully tease apart the clods, and the mycorrhizae will be there.

Left. **Eastern White Pine,** ***Pinus strobus***

This sample was dug in winter 1992 in New Hampshire. The root was in non-frozen soil directly below frozen soil. The mycorrhizae and root hairs were fresh. Common on winter-dug samples are jelly-like coatings of the root. The material appears to be made up of bacteria. Or they may be blue-green algae. There is no doubt that non-woody roots — root hairs, mycorrhizae — grow in non-frozen soil directly below frozen soil. The top of the tree may be dormant, but the bottom is very active. Fuel for these processes must come from stored energy in the roots.

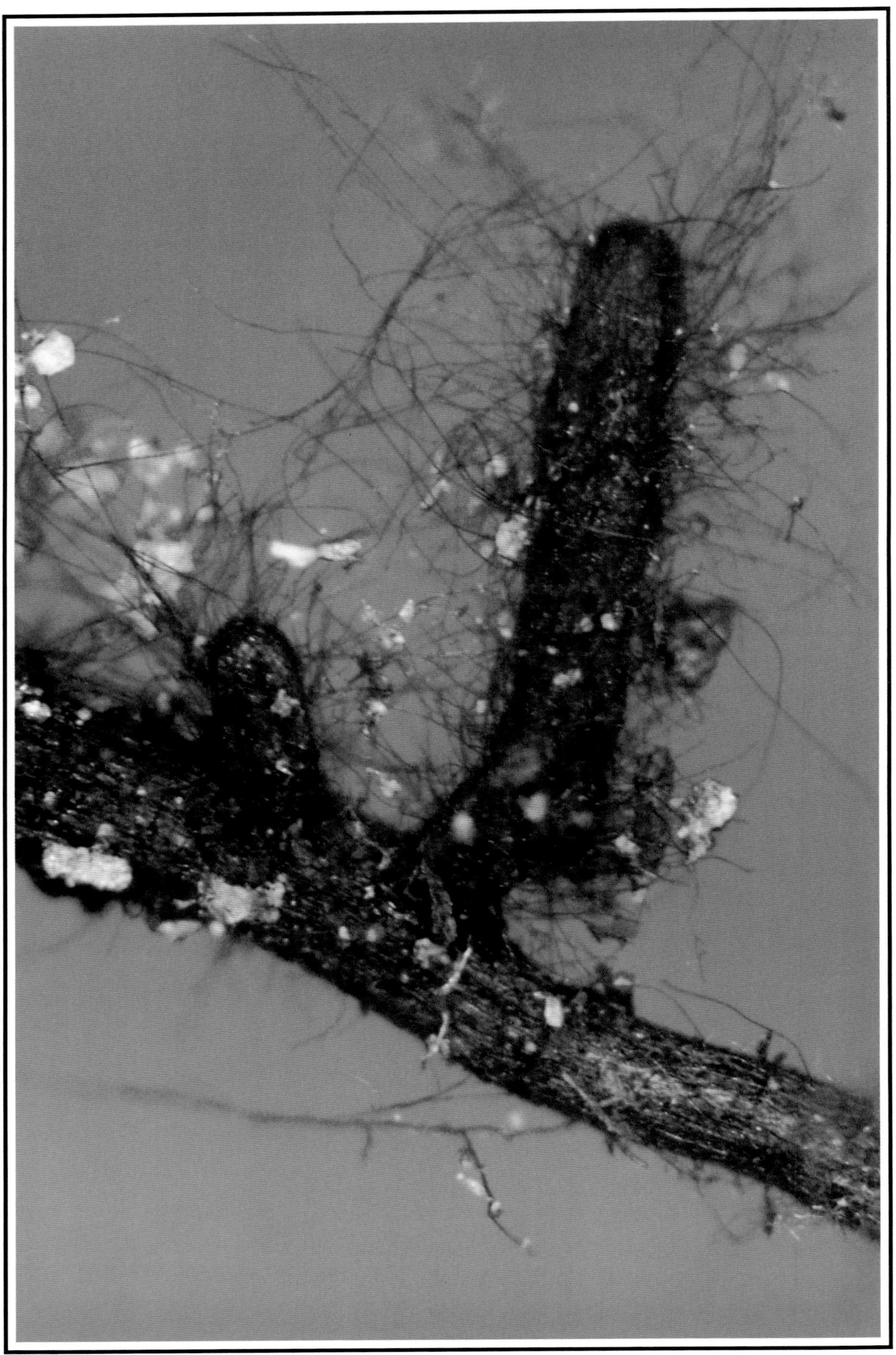

Black Mycorrhizae

There must be thousands of types of mycorrhizae. Here is a common black form that has hyphae growing out far beyond the mycorrhizae. Note again and again that so many mycorrhizae "stand up" in micro cavities in the soil. When the micro cavities are crushed, so are the mycorrhizae. It is common to have several to many different species of fungi associated with mycorrhizae on the same tree. There are some fungi that are specific to mycorrhizae on one species of tree.

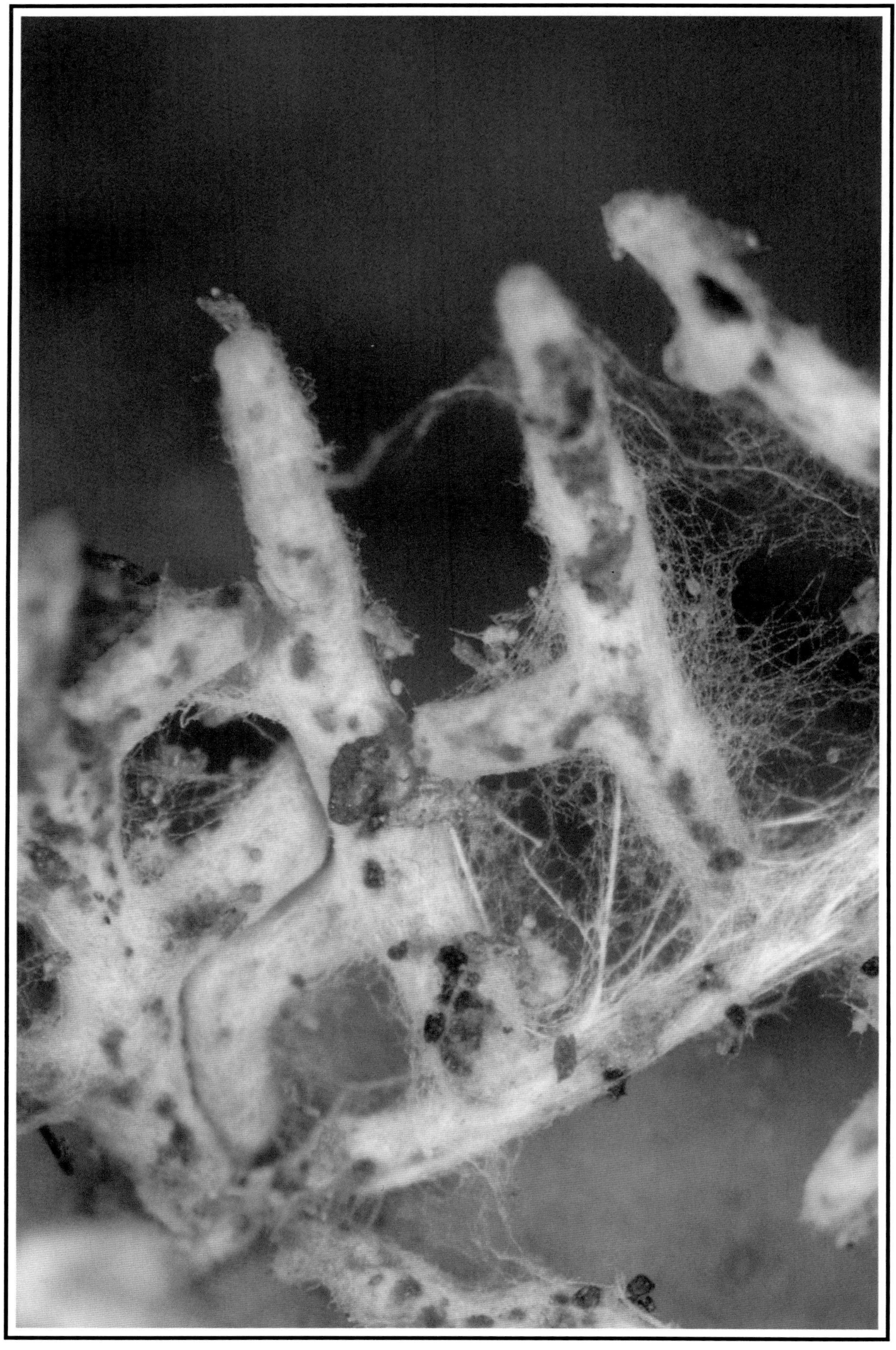

Mycorrhizae Covered With Hyphae

The mycorrhizae shown here are covered with fungus hyphae. If you were to calculate the amount of absorptive surface provided by all of the hyphae, the figures would boggle the mind. We must remember that what is shown on these pages is part of the tree system. When soils are compacted, this part of the tree system is destroyed. Yes, you can kill soil!

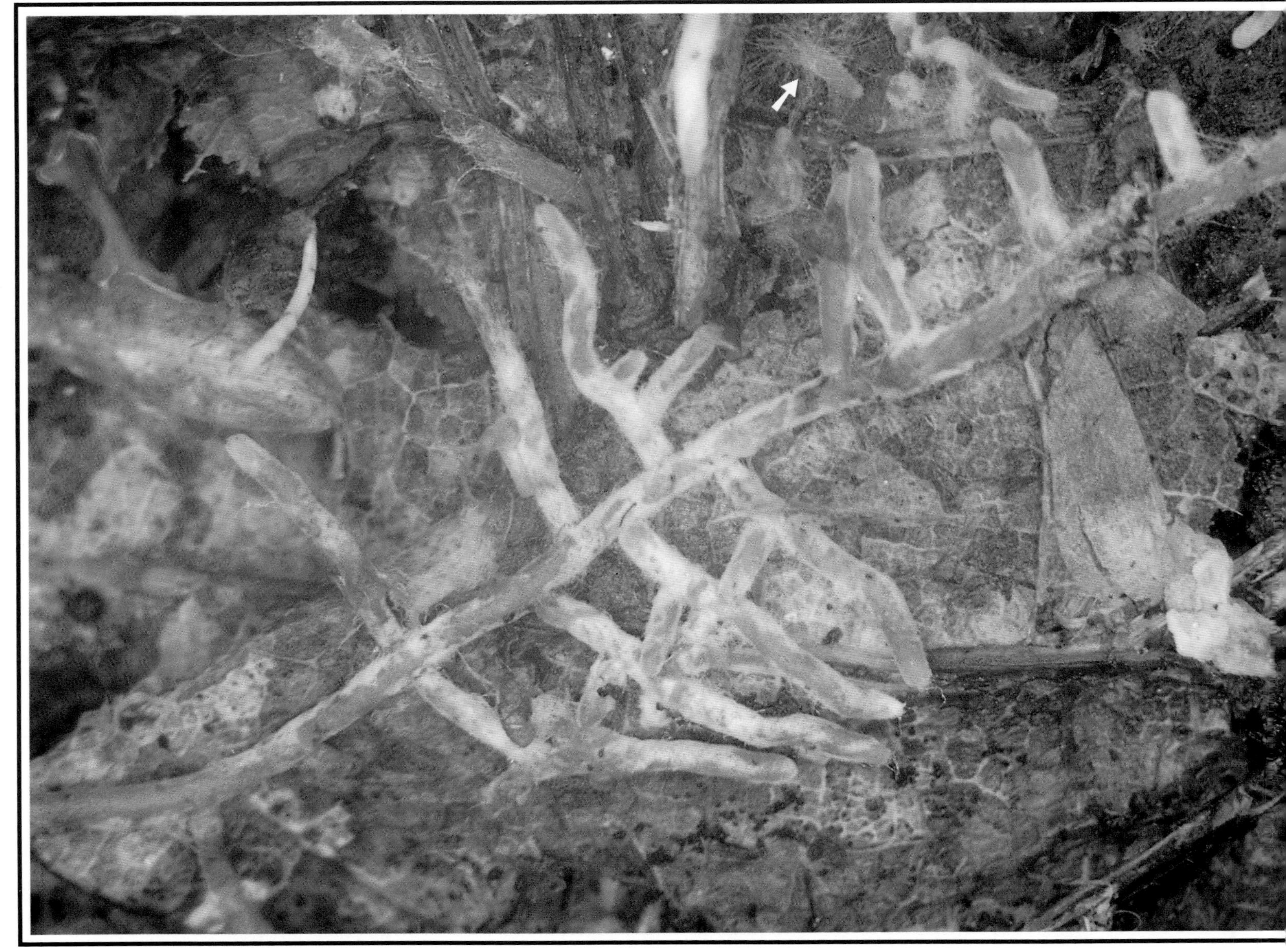

Mycorrhizae Between Leaves

Many types of mycorrhizae grow between sheets of dead leaves. This is how natural systems function to recycle many materials essential for life. The sheets of leaves were peeled off here to reveal an entire mycorrhiza. The fungus hyphae grew out too form a "velvet-like" coating over the entire structure. The arrow shows longer hyphae from another mycorrhiza. This is why dead leaves are so essential to the tree system. Natural systems recycle materials essential for life!

Right. **Two Types Of Mycorrhizae On The Same Root**

A few layers of leaves were pulled away from this sample after a gentle rain to show the two types of mycorrhizae on the same root. An entire, beautiful, majestic, wondrous world is there in the old leaves, twigs, and decaying branches and trunks. Again, this is all a part of the tree system. The recycling system.

I have found mycorrhizae commonly in dead leaves and in old down trunks that had brown rot. Brown rot is a type of rot where cellulose is digested and lignin is altered, but mostly left behind. I wonder if the fungi associated with some mycorrhizae are not able to digest lignin and get a carbon energy source from the old leaves and from brown rot.

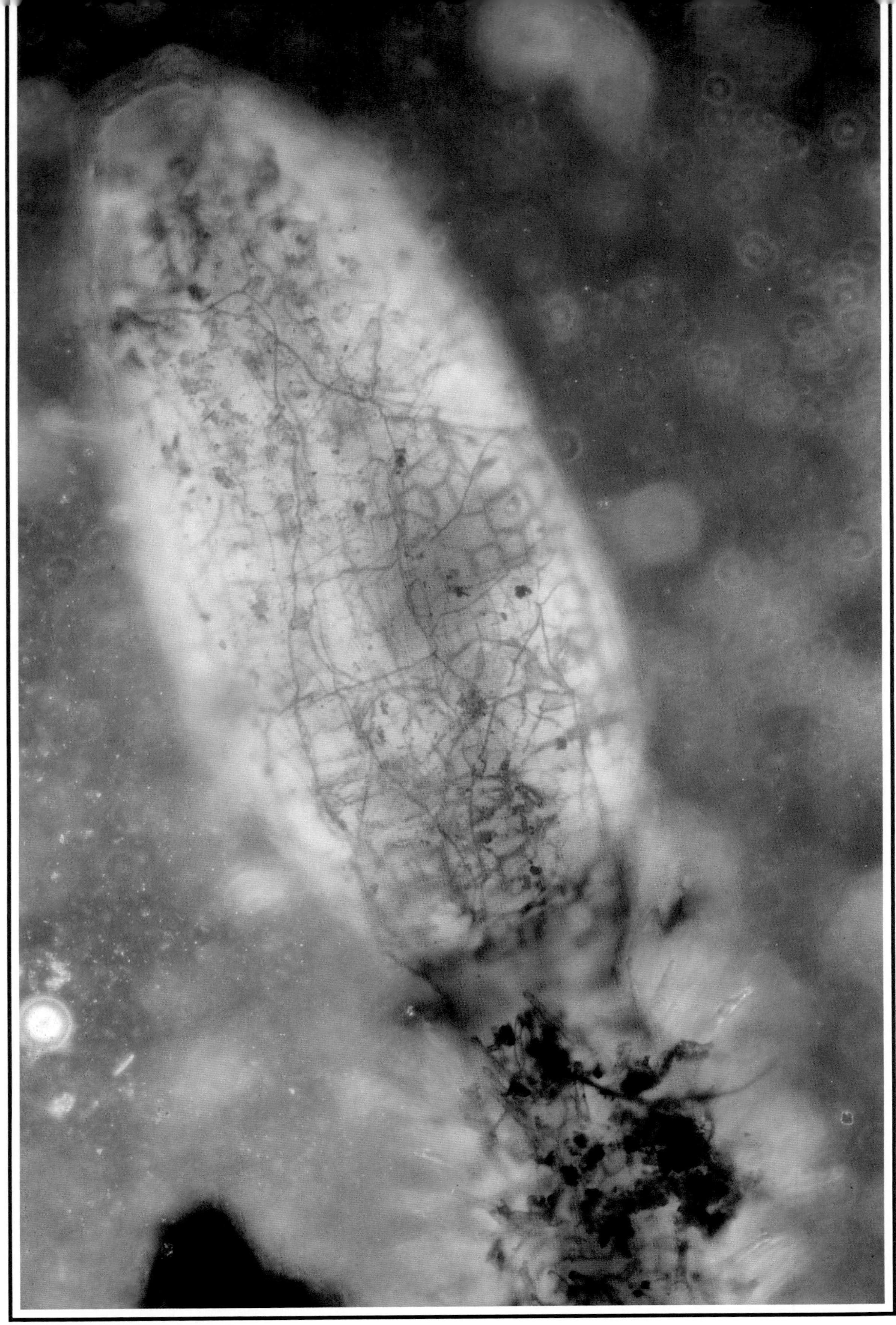

Hyphae Within A Mycorrhiza
Back lighting under a phase microscope shows the network of hyphae within a mycorrhiza. Toluidine blue was added to the sample. Note the root hairs at the base.

Right. **Hyphae Growing Out Of A Mycorrhiza**
Using the same procedures, this sample shows the hyphae as glass tubes projecting out of the mycorrhiza. The fungus-tree association is a symbiotic one. The fungi receive carbohydrates from the tree and the fungi facilitate the absorption of phosphorus and other elements for the tree.

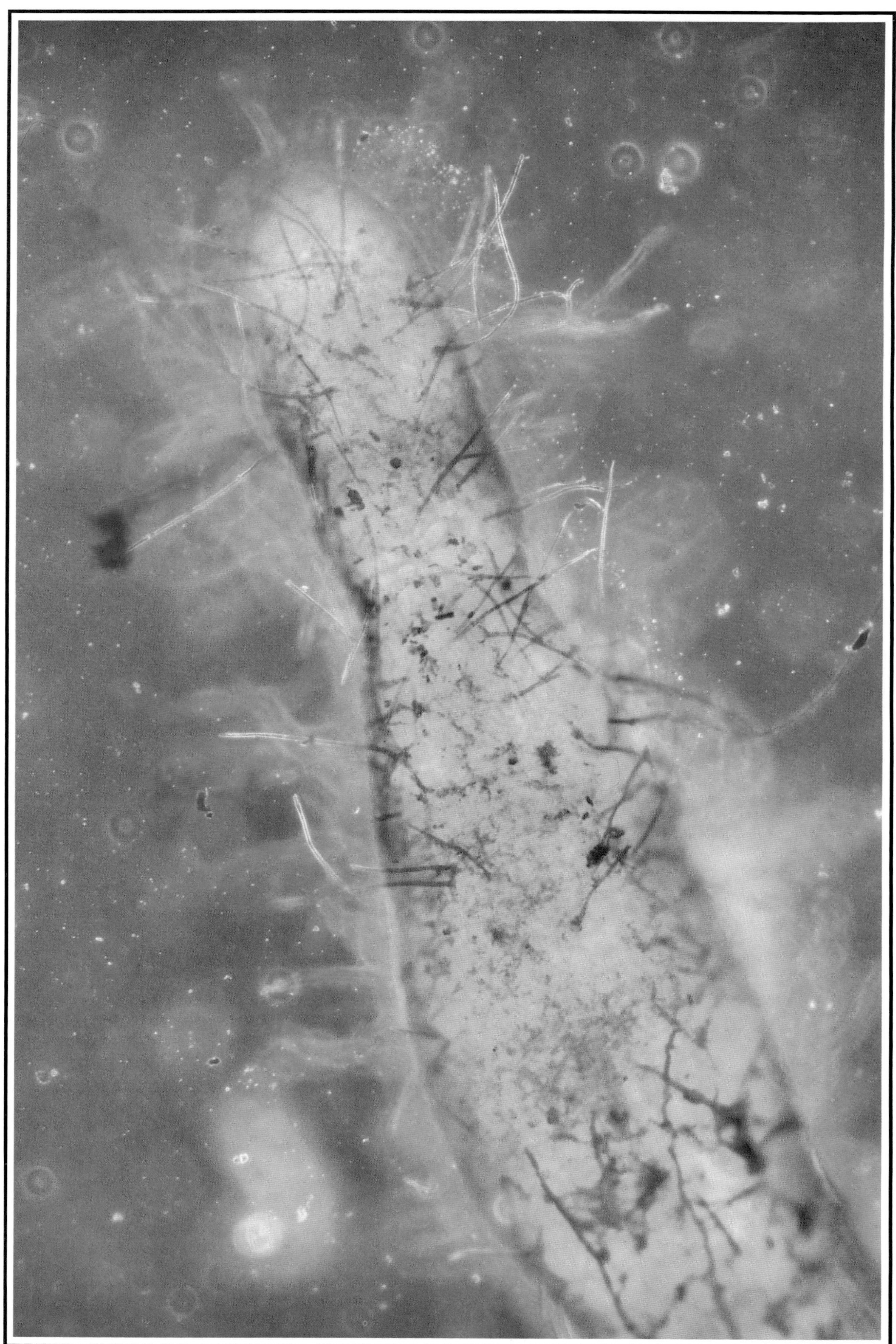

Xeromphalina sp.

The fungi play a major role in recycling essential elements from dead organic matter. The fungi often do this in association with many other organisms in the soil: bacteria, insects, worms, amoebae, nematodes, and small animals. The brilliantly colored minute mushrooms were fruit bodies of a fungus recycling elements in a dead log. Many of the fungi associated with mycorrhizae have mushroom fruit bodies. Others have a variety of fruit bodies above ground and below ground. The major point is that the members of the natural system are all connected. When the connections begin to be broken, the system will suffer. You can kill soil. You can kill a forest. You can kill many living things that depend on a healthy forest. How? By breaking connections.

Sweetfern, *Comptonia peregrina*

Actinorhizae on the root of sweetfern, *Comptonia peregrina.* Actinorhizae are organs composed of root tissue and actinomycetes. The actinorhizae fix nitrogen, which means that nitrogen in the air is converted to a form that can be used by the plant. Actinorhizae are common on trees in many genera, *Alnus, Elaeagnus, Casuarina,* to name a few. The actinomycetes are microorganisms that have some characteristics of fungi and bacteria. Actinomycetes give soil that "good earth smell". Bacterial nodules are common on many plants in the legume family. Nitrogen is fixed by bacteria in the nodules.

WOUND COMPARTMENTALIZATION

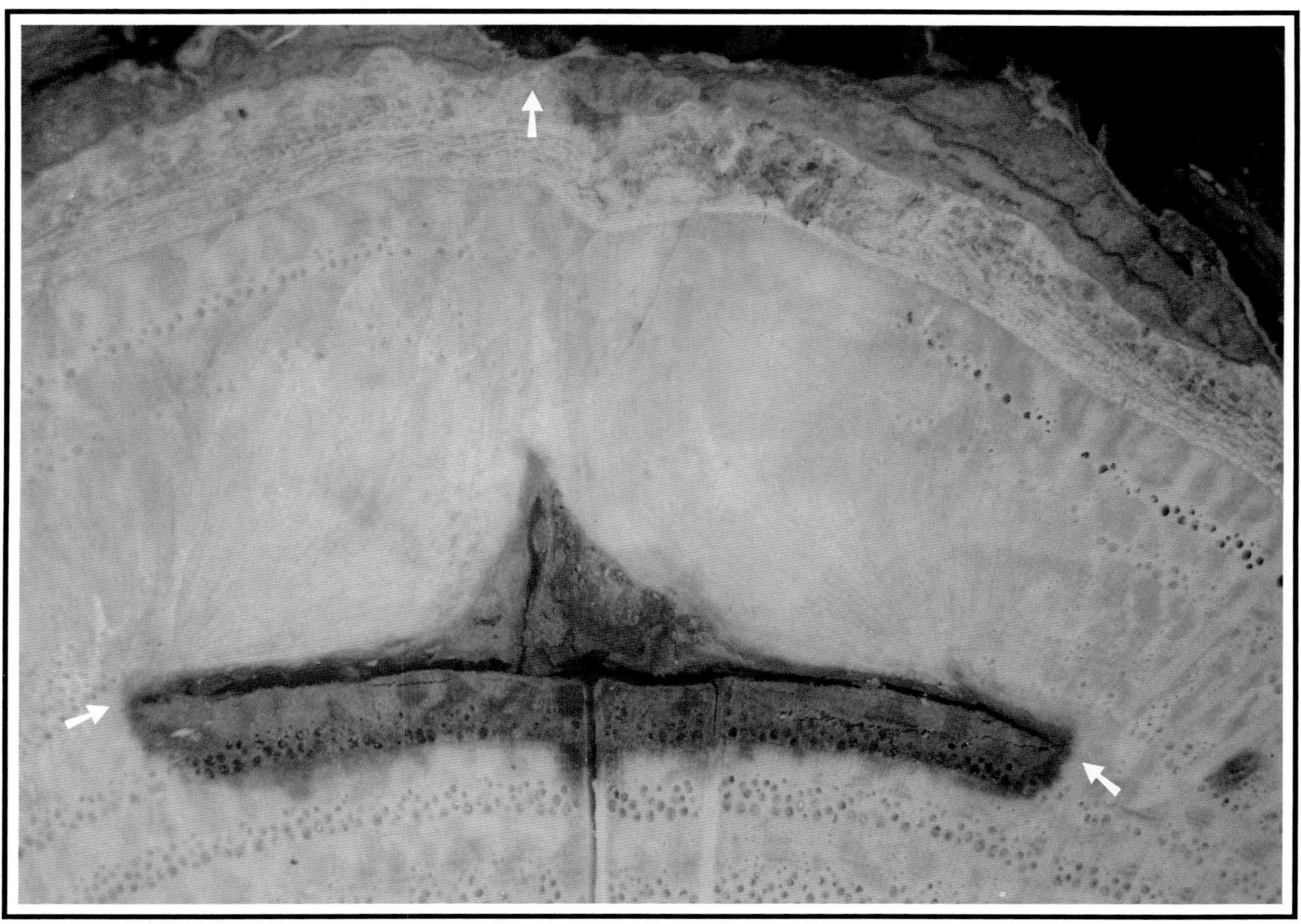

Bur Oak, *Quercus macrocarpa*

A small closed wound on an old tree. The wound was inflicted late in the growing period 4 years before the sample was cut. The arrows to the sides of the wound show that approximately three-quarters of the growth increment was completed when the wound was inflicted. This means that the wound was inflicted about the first week of July. When wounds are inflicted during the growth period they can be dated to within a week of the injury. The arrow in the bark shows green tissues still present from the new bark that closed the wound. Note that the wood that closed the wound has very few vessels. The wood that closes wounds is called woundwood, not callus. Callus does form first, but as lignin forms in the new cell walls, the new tissue is correctly called woundwood.

American Beech, *Fagus grandifolia*

Two small wounds in a young beech tree. The small wound in the center was well compartmentalized. Once wood tissues are injured they are not restored. The tissues are walled off. That is why wounds can be easily dated. The larger wound is also well compartmentalized, but the woundwood has not yet closed the wound. Note the abundance of chlorophyll in the woundwood.

Details on compartmentalization, callus, woundwood, and pathological anatomy are given in my books, **A New Tree Biology and Dictionary, Tree Pruning,** and **Modern Arboriculture.**

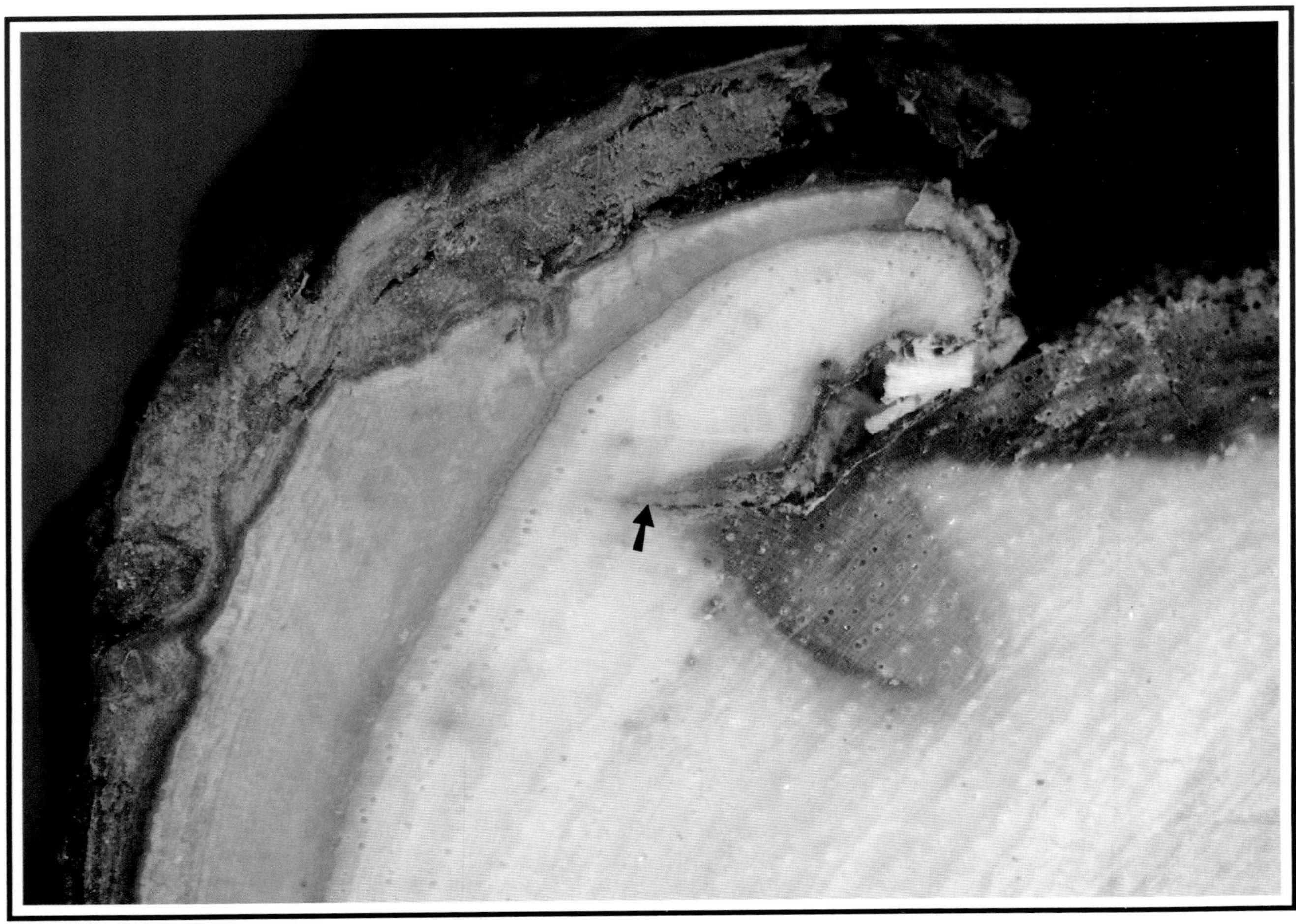

Shagbark Hickory, *Carya ovata*

When wounds close too rapidly, the woundwood often curls inward and an internal crack forms as shown by the arrow. Treatments and products that stimulate rapid wound closure often stimulate internal cracks to form. Once formed, the crack stays in the wood. The cracks may split outward when some other stimulus occurs such as a sudden impact, or sudden cold or heat. Note that a patch of discolored wood formed on the inner side of the crack also. When cracks form, discolored wood, and sometimes decayed wood, develops about the cracks.

When wounds with cracks are viewed later from cross sections of samples, it appears that the concept of compartmentalization is not correct because the defect has developed beyond the wound into new tissues that formed after the injury. It is the misunderstanding of internal cracks that has caused this confusion. It is the misunderstanding of internal cracks that keeps confusion alive about frost cracks and heat cracks.

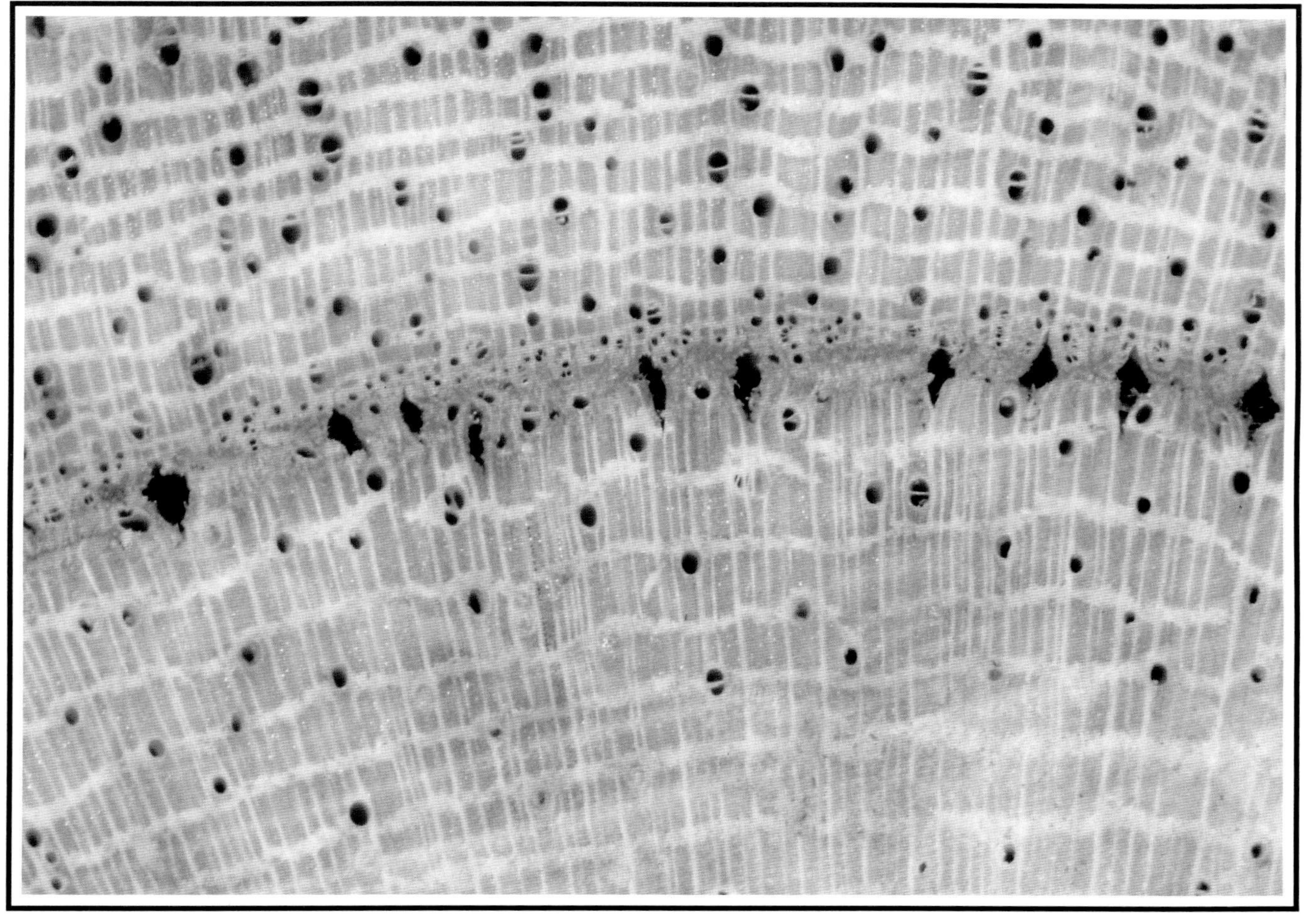

Fig, *Ficus microcarpa*

The brownish band of tissues with small cavities through the center of the photograph is a barrier zone. After wounding, the cambial zone that remains alive about the wound forms cells that differentiate to form a protection boundary called a barrier zone. The zone may be large or small, or almost nonexistent depending on the severity of the wound, time of wounding, and species of tree. Several wounds were inflicted at the same time about the trunk of the tree that yielded this sample. The small internal cracks in the barrier zone set the stage for more serious cracking later if other stimuli occur, such as sudden impact, drying, heat, or cold.

Phytolacca, ***Phytolacca dioica***

Tropical trees also form protection boundaries — reaction zone — after wounding. This tree was twisted and split by high winds during a hurricane. The sample was collected 6 months later. It was stained with iodine. The reaction zone was orange. It formed behind the wound and about the cracks. The lack of starch near the orange boundaries suggests that stored carbohydrate was used to form the protection boundaries. Forming a boundary is a defense action. Once formed, the boundary is then a protection feature. Xylem and phloem occur in bundles in the wood.

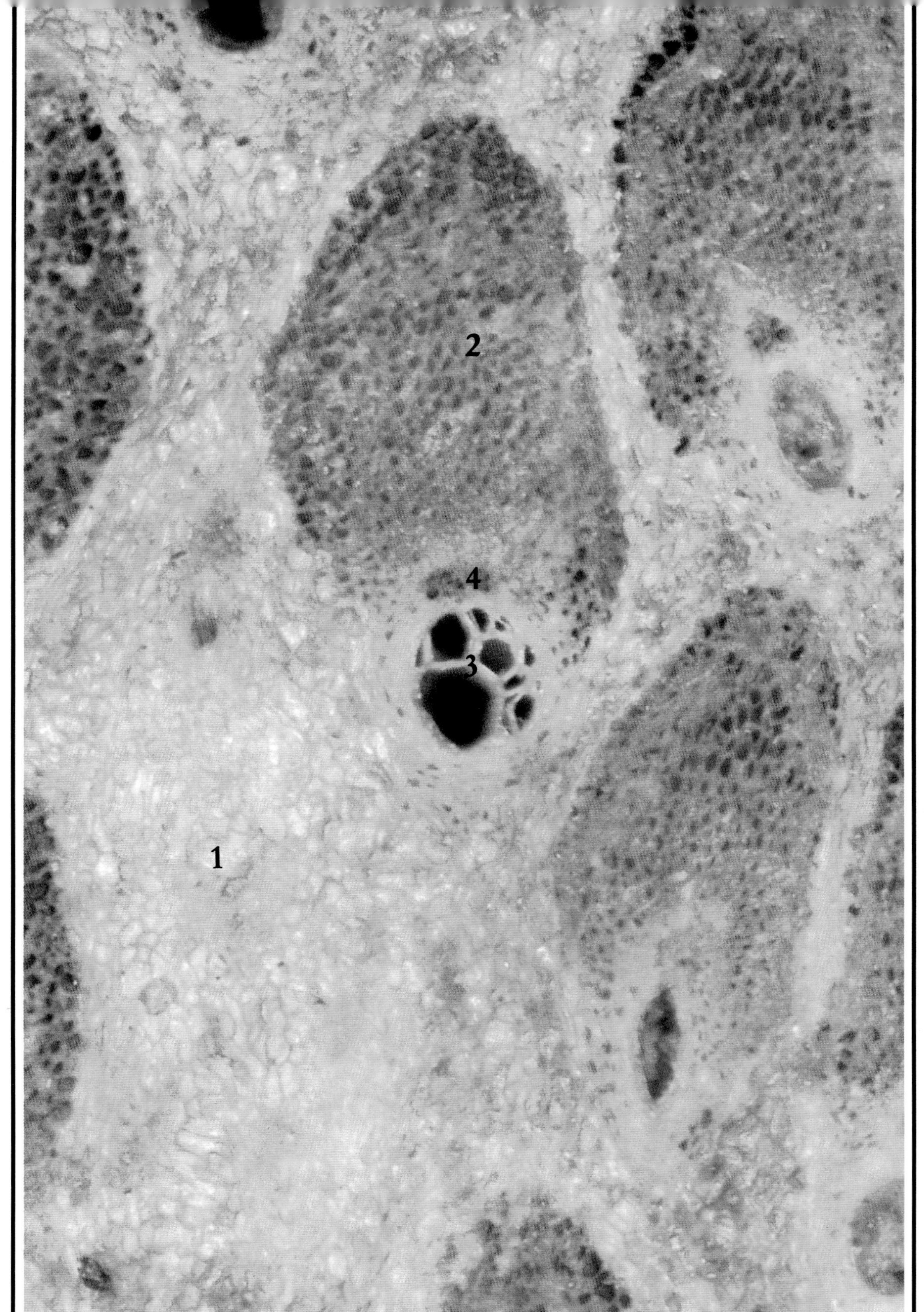

PALMS

Solitare Palm, *Ptychosperma elegans*

Palms are monocots; they are members of a group called monocotyledones. The seed has a single cotyledon or seed leaf, whereas the dicotyledones — oaks, maples, beech— have 2 seed leaves, or cotyledons. Palms have only apical meristems that extend their axial growth. Ground tissues (1) in the stem contain vascular bundles (2) with xylem (3) and phloem (4). As always in nature, there are exceptions. Some members of the monocots do have a type of secondary growth that expands their girth — *Cordyline* spp.

Tissues injured by wounds are walled off in palms.

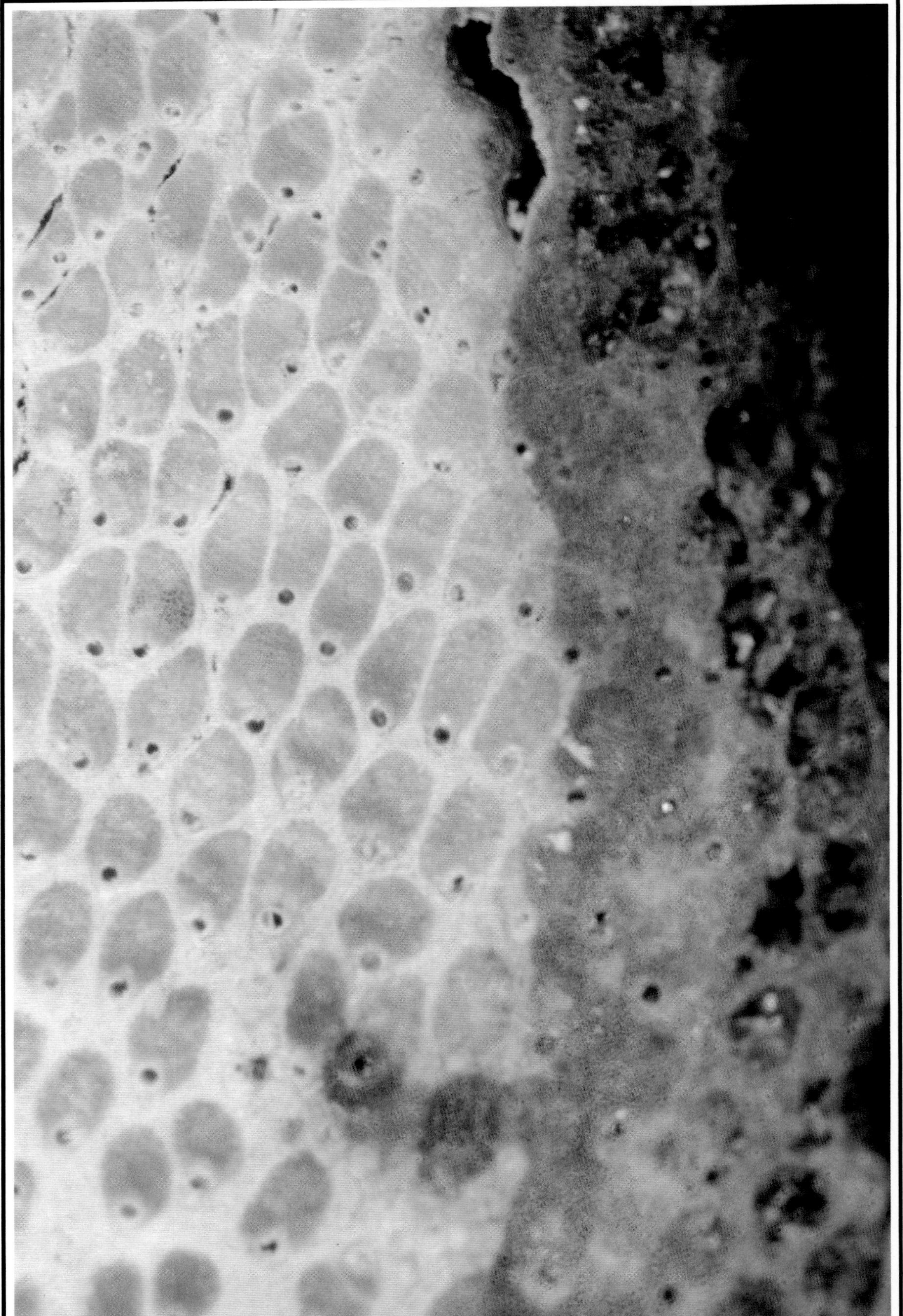

Solitare Palm, *Ptychosperma elegans*

After wounding , vascular bundles are altered in ways that seal off, or wall off the injured tissues from the inner healthy tissues. The darker tissues on the right side of this photograph were killed by a fire.

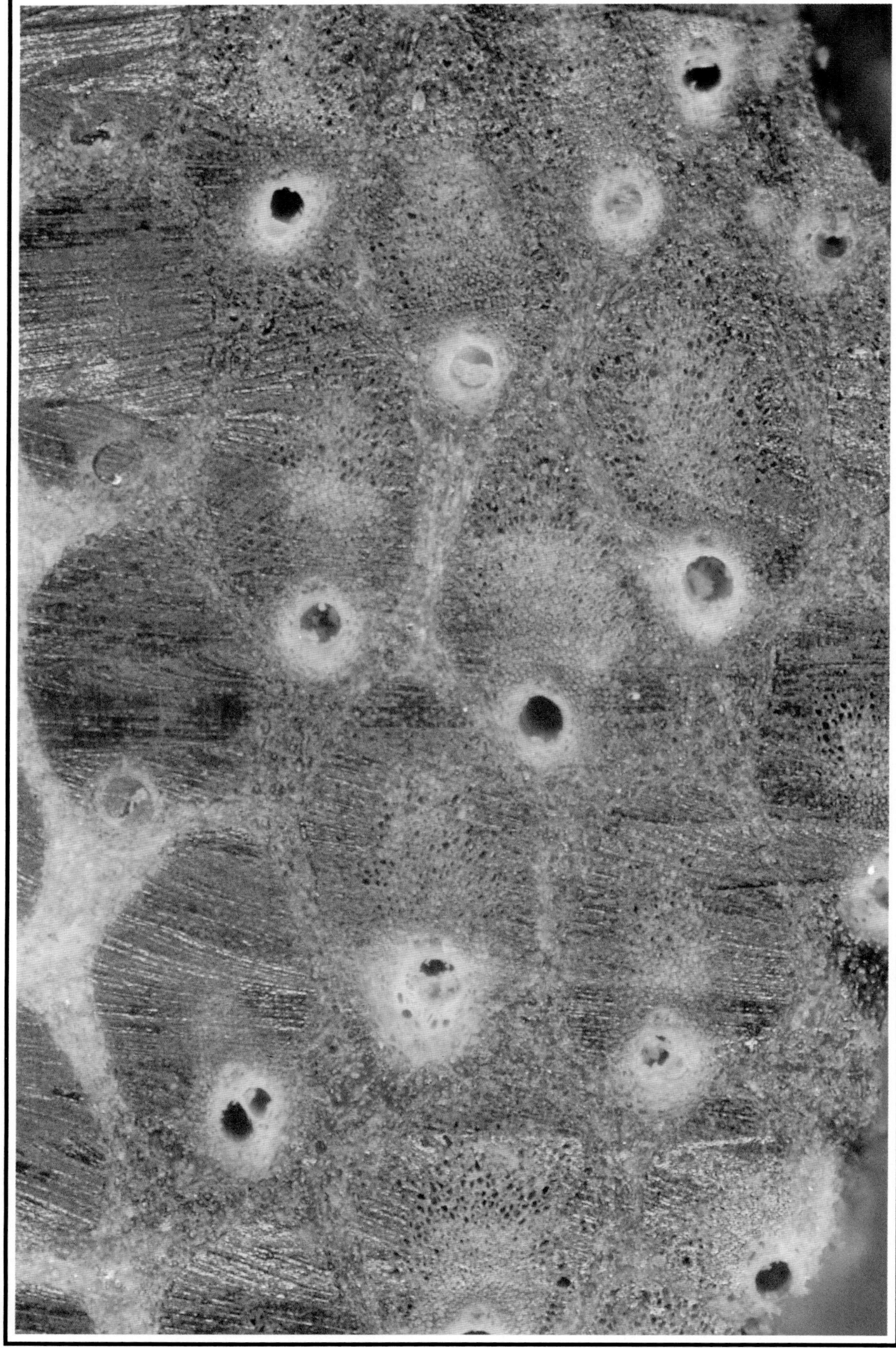

Boundary zones form after wounding in palms.

Solitare Palm, *Ptychosperma elegans*
A closer view of the boundary of altered tissues that walled off the dead tissues shown on the previous page. Some palms form boundaries of altered tissues much faster and much more effectively than palms in other genera. For example, wounds in coconut palm, *Cocos nucifera* are walled off much more effectively than wounds in royal palm, *Roystonea regia.* Studies on dicot trees have shown that compartmentalization is under moderate to strong genetic control. The same may be true for monocot trees.

WOOD GROWTH IN TROPICAL TREES

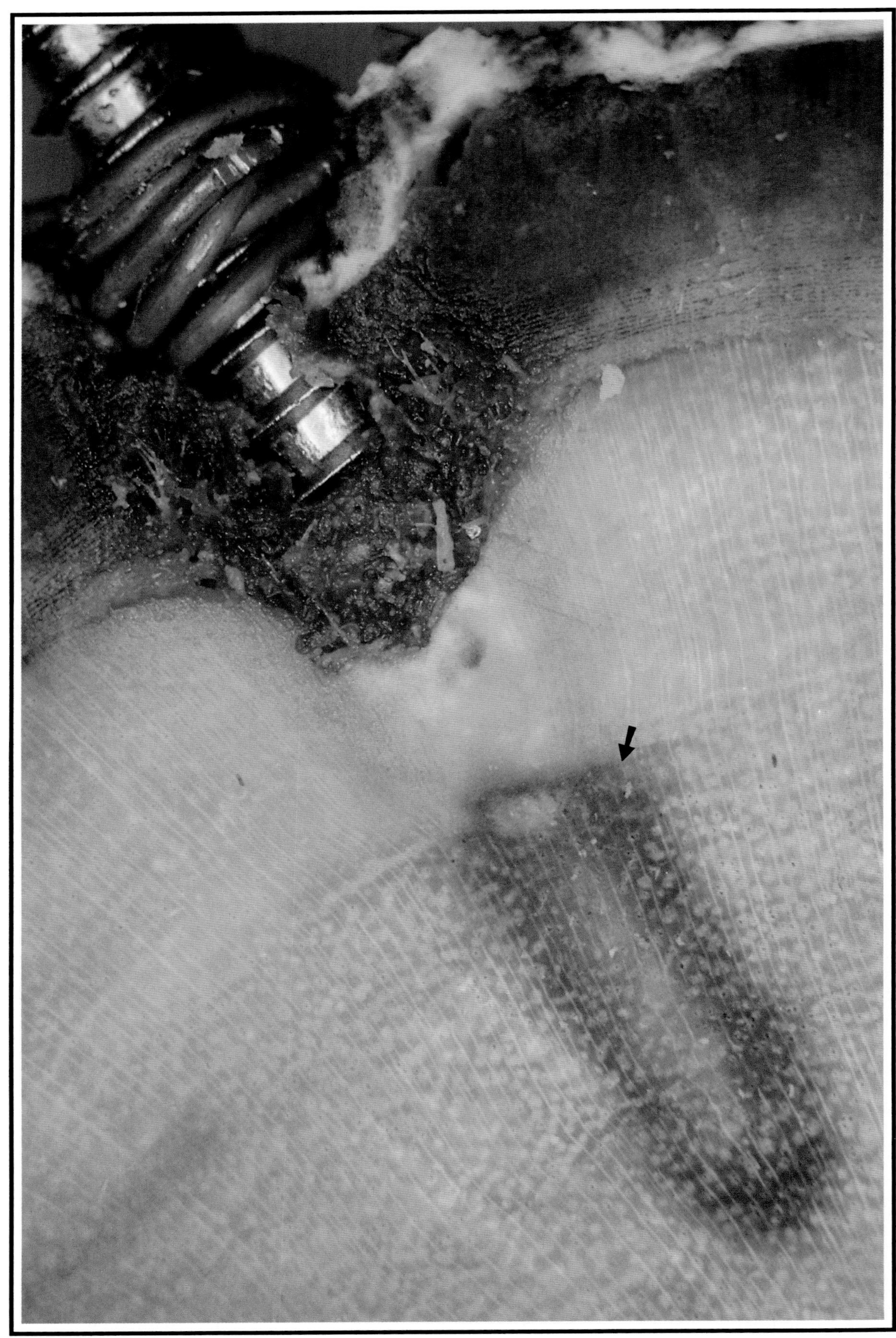

Tung Tree, ***Aleurites fordii***

Because many tropical trees do not have obvious growth increments, studies are now in progress to determine exactly when some tropical trees are growing wood. Screws have been inserted into the trees at recorded calendar dates. After a year, the trees are cut and examined, or the tree can remain alive and increment cores can be taken to examine the wood. Because trees compartmentalize injured tissues, the exact position of the wood at the time of injury by the screw will be seen (arrow). A tag indicating date of wounding is attached to the screw by copper wire.

SUMMARY

1. Tree anatomy is beautiful and majestic.
2. Flowers on most trees have both male and female parts — perfect flowers, monoclinous.
3. Some trees have male and female flowers — on separate trees, dioecious; on the same tree, monoecious; diclinous.
4. Some seeds have embryos that grow after the seed matures and falls while other seeds pass through a dormant period.
5. Stored energy is required for development of new leaves.
6. Before chlorophyll forms in a leaf, the leaf could be a color other than green depending on the first pigments that formed.
7. As leaves die, chlorophyll is no longer produced, and the leaf takes on colors of the other pigments present.
8. Many insects and mites feed and breed on leaves.
9. Starch is stored behind buds during the end of the growing season.
10. On some trees, smaller buds form to the sides of larger buds. The smaller buds may remain dormant for several growing periods.
11. The pith of branches does not connect directly with the pith of the stem.
12. Chlorophyll is usually abundant in the cortex, pith, or other living tissues in young twigs.
13. Current growth has a thin covering of epidermis. The one-year-old twigs have a thin covering called a primary periderm.
14. Most oak species have a star-shaped pith.
15. Chlorophyll is abundant in living parenchyma cells in young trees of most species.
16. Reaction wood forms when trees lean. Compression wood forms on the lower side of the lean in conifers. Tension wood forms on the upper side of the lean in woody angiosperms.
17. Green, cortex-like tissues are common under the periderm in young trees of many species.
18. Xylem rays connect radially to form phloem rays. The phloem rays connect circumferentially to form the phellogen.
19. Ring-porous trees have large earlywood vessels and smaller vessels in latewood.
    Diffuse-porous trees have vessels, usually small, of approximately the same size scattered evenly throughout the growth increment.
20. Free water moves only in the latewood of the current increment during the end of the growth period in some tyloses-forming species of ring-porous trees such as American elm.
21. Plane trees store an abundance of starch in broad rays. Plane trees maintain a thick green cortex-like layer under the outer bark on mature trees. The phellem is shed every growth period and the green layer is exposed. Many other tree species have a similar mechanism for maintaining a cortex-like layer on aging trunks.
22. Layers of green cortex-like tissues often form in fissures on old trees that have thick bark.
23. Sapwood is wood that has living cells. Sapwood in many tree species maintains only a single growth increment that has open vessels. A distinction needs to be made between sapwood that is conducting and sapwood that is not conducting.
24. Live oaks have vessel patterns that are similar to those in latewood of other oaks. Live oaks have very broad rays.
25. The current developing growth increment does not store starch until the end of the growth period.
26. Sapwood has an interconnected network of living axial and radial parenchyma.
27. The symplast is the network of connected living cells; axial and radial parenchyma in wood, the cambial zone, living cells in the inner phloem, phloem rays, and the phellogen.
28. The apoplast is the framework of non-living cells and cell walls in wood and bark.
29. The newly formed vessels do not become functional until the end walls or septa between the vessel cells rupture.
30. When trees are stressed, only earlywood may form.
31. Tyloses are structures produced by the living axial parenchyma that plug the vessels. Once formed, the tyloses stay in place.
32. Vessels curve and join with other vessels as seen in a longitudinal view. Vessels do end.
33. Conifers have tracheids. Woody angiosperms have vessels.
34. Widths of growth increments decrease when trees are stressed.
35. Some tropical trees have bands of phloem-like tissues within the xylem.
36. Woody roots on most trees do not have a pith. Woody roots usually store more energy reserves than stems.
37. Callus is a tissue that is meristematic, low in lignin, and homogenous as to cell types. Woundwood is not meristematic, is high in lignin, and has differentiated cells — vessels, fibers, axial and radial parenchyma.
38. Meristematic points are sheets of radial parenchyma that extend from the wood into the outer bark. The points have the capacity to form sprouts, flowers, woody roots, and prop roots.
39. Root hairs are extensions of epidermal cells on non-woody roots.
40. Non-woody roots shed dying and dead root hairs and epidermal cells. The shed cells are digested by soil microorganisms. They recycle elements essential for life.
41. Mycorrhizae form when some fungi infect young, emerging non-woody roots. The mycorrhizae are organs made up of tree and fungus tissues. The organs facilitate the absorption of phosphorus, manganese, copper, and zinc.
42. Many mycorrhizae grow in micro cavities in the soil. Compaction destroys the micro cavities.
43. Mycorrhizae and root hairs often grow in non-frozen soils directly below frozen soils.
44. Hyphae of the fungus associated with a mycorrhiza often grow out beyond the mycorrhiza into the soil.
45. Some mycorrhizae grow between old, dead leaves, and in brown-rotted wood suggesting that the fungi may be able to digest lignin.
46. Actinorhizae are structures made up of tree tissues and actinomycetes. They fix nitrogen.
47. Wounded wood is compartmentalized in trees.
48. After wounding, callus forms first about the margins of the wound. Woundwood forms later as the cells become lignified.
49. When wounds close rapidly, the woundwood often curls inward and forms internal cracks.
50. Wounds are compartmentalized in tropical trees including palms.

RECYCLING

Many members of the tree system contribute to the survival of the system by recycling elements essential for life, from dead parts of the system.

The small mushrooms shown above are fruit bodies of the fungi that are growing on dead needles.

On page 100 a yellow slime mold is growing on dead leaves.

On page 101 another type of slime mold, *Lycogala epidendrum,* is shown on an old decaying log. The spore-bearing structures are red when young, and brown when mature.

Slime molds are organisms that have some characteristics of fungi and amoebae. They usually grow on dead organic matter that is in the advanced stage of breakdown.

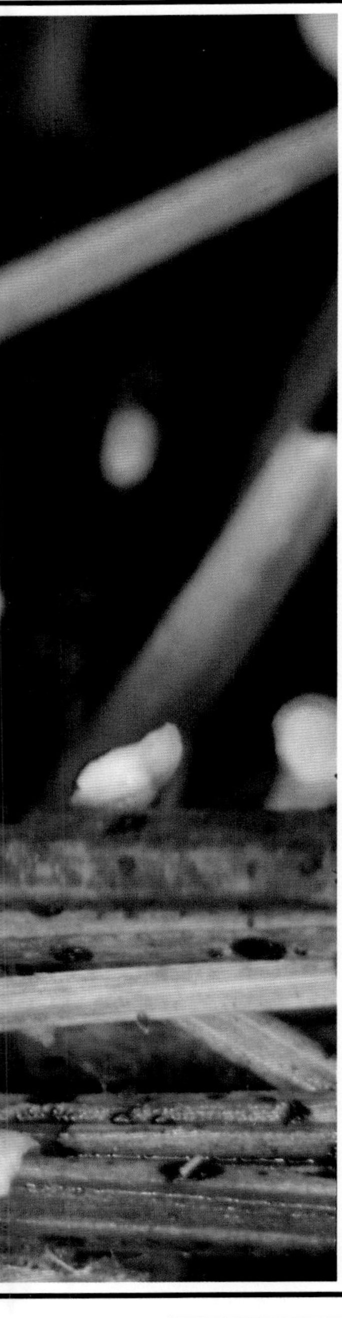

CONNECTIONS

DECISIONS SURVIVAL UNDERSTANDING

TREE ANATOMY is about the parts and structures of the tree system and their connections.

The parts are not only the tissues but also the members of the system.

The structures are not only the arrangements of tissues, but also the connections of the members of the system.

Each member is made up of parts and structures. All members are connected to make up the tree system.

The tree system is beautiful and majestic, not only because of its colors and shapes, but because of the way it is connected.

All connected members contribute something to the system that helps to ensure its long-term high- quality survival.

Some members are part of the buildup processes. Others are part of the breakdown processes.

You cannot say that one part of the system is more important than another part. They are all important for the survival of the system.

The dynamic equilibrium of the system is maintained by the continuing processes of buildup and breakdown.

Decisions on management of tree systems of the world are now concerns of many of the peoples of the world.

An understanding of the tree system is absolutely essential for making correct decisions that will ensure the long-term high-quality survival of the tree systems of the world.

BIBLIOGRAPHY

Here are some books and papers I suggest for further reading. They were very helpful to me in developing this book.

Baker, W.L. 1972. Eastern forest insects. US Dept. Agric. Forest Service, Misc. Publ. No. 1175, 642 p.

Bakshi, B.K. 1976. Forest Pathology. Controller of Publications, Delhi, 400 pp

Biggs, A.R. 1984. Boundary-zone formation in peach bark in response to wounds and *Cytospora leucostoma* infection. Can. J. Bot. 62: 2814-2821.

Broschat, T.K. and H.M. Donselman. 1984. Root regeneration in transplanted palms. Principles 28: 90-91, Florida Agric. Exp. Sta. J. Series No. 4694.

Burroughs, G.E. 1990. Anatomical aspects of root bud development in hoop pine (*Araucaria cunninghamii*). Aust. J. Bot. 38: 73-78.

Chudnoff, M. 1971. Tissue regeneration of debarked eucalypts. Forest Sci. 17: 300-305.

Del Tredici, P. 1992. Natural regeneration of *Ginkgo biloba* from downward growing cotyledonary buds (basal chichi). Amer. J. Bot. 79: 522-530.

Eames, A.J. and L.H. MacDaniels.1947. An Introduction to Plant Anatomy. McGraw-Hill Book Company, Inc. New York and London. 427 pp.

Eckstein, D., W. Liese, and A.L. Shigo. 1979. Relationship of wood structure to compartmentalization of discolored wood in hybrid poplar. Can J. For. Res. 9: 205-210.

Elias, T.S. 1980. The Complete Trees of North America. Outdoor Life/Nature Books, Van Nostrand Reinhold Co. New York. 948 pp.

Esau, K. 1965. Plant anatomy. 2nd ed. John Wiley & Sons, New York, London and Sydney.

Fahn, A. and B. Leshem. 1962. Wood fibres with living protoplasts. New Phytol. 62: 91-98.

Fisher, J.B. 1981. Wound healing by exposed secondary xylem in Adansonia (Bombacaceae). IAWA Bull. n.s. 2: 193-199.

Fisher, J.B. 1975. Eccentric secondary growth in *Cordyline* and other *Agavaceae.* (Monocotyledonae) and its correlation with auxin distribution. Amer. J. Bot. 62: 292-302.

Fisher, J.B. and J.W. Stevenson. 1981. Occurrence of reaction wood in branches of Dicotyledens and its role in tree architecture. Bot. Gaz. 142: 82-95.

Good, H.M., Murray, P.M., and H.M. Dale. 1955. Studies on heartwood formation and staining in sugar maple. Can. J. Bot. 33: 31-41.

Gregory, R.A. 1978. Living elements of the conducting secondary xylem of sugar maple (Acer saccharum Marsh.). IAWA Bull. 4: 65-69

Grozdits, G.A., S.E. Godkin, and C.T. Keith. 1982. The periderms of three North American conifers. Part 1: Anatomy. Wood Sci. Technol. 16: 305-316.

Hacskaylo, E. (ed). 1971. Mycorrhizae. Proc. First N. Amer. Conf. on Mycorrhizae. US Dept. Agric. Forest Service Misc. Publ. 1189. 255.

Haissig, B.E. and R.E. Dickson. 1979. Starch measurement in plant tissues using enzymatic hydrolysis. Physiol. Plant. 47: 151-157.

Hardwick, R.C. 1987. The nitrogen content of plants and the self-thinning rule of plant ecology: A test of the core-skin hypothesis. Ann. Bot. 60: 439-446.

Head, G.C. 1973. Shedding of roots. 237-293. in Shedding of Plant Parts. T. Kozlowski (ed), Academic Press. New York. 560 p.

Hejnowicz, Z. and J.A. Romberger. 1979. The common basis of wood grain figures is the systematically changing orientation of cambial fusiform cells. Wood Sci. and Technol. 13: 89-96.

Hillis, W.E. 1977. Secondary changes in wood. Recent Advances in Phytochemistry 11: 247-309. F.A. Loewus and V.C. Runeckles (eds), Plenum Publ. Corp. New York.

Hyland, F. 1974. Fiber analysis and distribution in the leaves, juvenile stems and roots of the Maine trees and shrubs. Univ. Maine, Tech. Bull. 71. 68 p.

Johnson, W.T. and H.H. Lyon. 1991. Insects That Feed On Trees and Shrubs. Comstock Publishing Associates, a division of Cornell University Press, Ithaca and London. 560 pp.

Jorgensen, E. 1962. Observations on the formation of protection wood. Forestry Chronicle 38: 292-294.

Kribs, D.A. 1968. Commercial Foreign Woods on the American Market. Dover Publ., Inc., New York. 241 p.

Küster, E. 1925. Pathologische Pflanzenanatomie, 3. Aufl. Verlag G. Fisher, Jena. 558 p. (English translation in Library of Univ. Wisconsin, and Forest Insect and Disease lab. Hamden, Connecticut.)

MacDougal, D.T. and G.M. Smith. 1927. Long-lived cells of the redwood. Science 66: 456-457.

Mattheck, C. 1991. Trees. The Mechanical Design. Springer-Verlag New York, Berlin. 121 pp.

Mayer-Wegelin, H. 1936. Ästung. Verlag M.V.H. Schaper, Hannover.

McCurrach, J.C. 1960. Palms of the world. 1980 reprint by Horticultural Books, Inc. Stuart, Florida.

Molina, R. and J.M. Trappe. 1984. Mycorrhiza management in bareroot nurseries. 211-223. in Duryea, M.L. and T.D. Landis (eds). Forest Nursery Manual: Production of Bareroot Seedlings. Martinus Nijhof/Dr. W. Junk Publishers. The Hague/Boston/Lancaster.

Mullick, D.B. 1977. The non-specific nature of defense in bark and wood during wounding, insect and pathogen attack. Recent Advances in Phytochemistry 11: 395-441. in F.A. Loewus and V.C. Runeckle (eds). Plenum Publishing Corp. New York.

Perry, T.O. 1989. Tree roots: Facts and fallacies. Arnoldia 49: 3-21.

Persson, H. 1979. Fine-root production, mortality and decomposition in forest ecosystems. Vegetatio 41:L 101-109.

Peterson, C.A. 1989. Significance of the exodermis in root function. in, B.C. Loughman et al. (eds). Structural and functional aspects of transport in roots, 35-40 (Kluwer Academic Publ.).

Phelps, J.E., E.A. McGinnes, Jr., and P.J-Y. Lieu. 1975. Anatomy of xylem tissue formation associated with radial seams and cracks in black oak. Wood Science 8: 397-405.

Raven, P.H., R.F. Evert, and S.E. Eichhorn. 1986. Biology of Plants. Worth Publ., Inc. New York. 775 p.

Schweingruber, F.H. 1982. Microscopic wood anatomy. F. Flück-Wirth, Switzerland, 226 p.

Sharon, E.M. 1973. Some histological features of *Acer saccharum* wood formed after wounding. Can. J. For. Res. 3: 83-89.

Shortle, W.C. 1979. Mechanisms of compartmentalization of decay in living trees. Phytopathology 69: 1147-1151.

Sinclair, W.A., H.H. Lyon, and W.T. Johnson. 1987. Diseases of trees and shrubs. Comstock Publ. Assoc., Div. of Cornell Univ. Press, Ithaca, 574 p.

Siau, J.F. 1984. Transport processes in wood. Springer-Verlag, Berlin, Heidelberg, New York, Tokyo. 245 p.

Srivastava, L.M. 1964. Anatomy, chemistry, and physiology of bark. Inter. Rev. For. Res. 1: 203-277. Academic Press. New York.

Tippet, J.T. 1982. Shedding of ephemeral roots in gymnosperms. Can. J. Bot. 60: 2295-2302.

Tippett, J.T., 1986. Formation and fate of kino veins in Eucalyptus L'Hérit. IAWA Bull. n.s. 7: 137-143.

Tomlinson, P.B. 1986. The Biology of Trees Native to Tropical Florida. Harvard University Printing Office, Allston, Massachusetts. 480 pp.

Tomlinson, P.B.. 1990. The Structural Biology of Palms. Clarendon Press Oxford. 477 pp.

von Aufsess, H. 1975. The formation of a protective zone at the base of branches of broadleafed and coniferous trees and its effectiveness in preventing fungi from penetrating into the heartwood of living trees. Forstwiss. Cbl. 94: 14-152.

Walter, K.E.. 1968. A new method for marking xylem growth. Forest Science 14: 102-104.

Wargo, P.M. 1975. Estimating starch content in roots of deciduous trees — a visual technique. US Dept. Agric. Forest Service Res. Paper NE-313, 9 p.

Wargo, P.W. 1971. Seasonal changes in carbohydrate levels in roots of sugar maple. US Dept. Agric. Forest Service Res. Paper NE-213, 8 p.

Worral, J.J. and J.R. Parmeter. 1983. Inhibition of wood decay fungi by wetwood of white fir. Phytopathology 73: 1140-1145.

Zabel, R.A. and J.J. Morrell. 1992. Wood Microbiology. Academic Press, Inc. New York. 476 pp.

Zimmerman, M.H. 1979. The discovery of tyloses formation by a Viennese lady in 1845. IAWA Bull. 2-3:51-56.

Zimmerman, M.H. 1983. Xylem Structure and the Ascent of Sap. Springer-Verlag, Berlin, Heidelberg, New York, and Tokyo.

Zimmerman, M.H. and C.L. Brown. 1980. Tree Structure and Function. Springer-Verlag, New York, Heidelberg, and Berlin.

INDEX

SPECIES SHOWN IN PHOTOGRAPHS

TREES AND OTHER ORGANISMS MENTIONED BUT NOT SHOWN

Carol Phelps